Table of Contents

Introduction

“牛津技能世界：英语听说专项训练”系列将英语听力和英语口语的学习以灵活有趣的方式结合到一起，着眼于策略和技巧的教授，有助于学生自主学习并达成学习目标。

快来开启你的探险之旅吧!

大家好，我们是奥利和莫莉，也是牛津技能世界探险之旅的向导。我们会讲授实用的听力和口语学习策略，提出有针对性的问题并给出合理的建议，帮助你达成学习目标。相信在我们的陪伴下，你的探险之旅将充满乐趣！还在等什么？快开始吧！

LISTENING WITH SPEAKING

牛津技能世界
英语听说专项训练3

［英］吉尔·科里·奥沙利文◎著　石若琳◎译

北京科学技术出版社
100层童书馆

著作权合同登记号　图字：01-2023-5634

图书在版编目（CIP）数据

牛津技能世界．英语听说专项训练 3 /（英）吉尔·科里·奥沙利文著；石若琳译．-- 北京：北京科学技术出版社，2025. -- ISBN 978-7-5714-4475-4

Ⅰ. G624. 313

中国国家版本馆 CIP 数据核字第 2025NN2055 号

策划编辑：闫　娉
责任编辑：樊川燕
封面设计：包荧莹
图文制作：史维肖
责任印制：吕　越
出 版 人：曾庆宇
出版发行：北京科学技术出版社
社　　址：北京西直门南大街16号
邮政编码：100035
ISBN 978-7-5714-4475-4

电　　话：0086-10-66135495（总编室）
　　　　　0086-10-66113227（发行部）
网　　址：www.bkydw.cn
印　　刷：雅迪云印（天津）科技有限公司
开　　本：889 mm × 1194 mm　1/16
字　　数：165千字
印　　张：8.25
版　　次：2025年3月第1版
印　　次：2025年3月第1次印刷

定　　价：91.50元

Quick Guide

引入话题

话题贴近学生生活，且都基于特定的主题。

这里列出了每个单元*的学习目标。

奇闻趣事
旨在快速激发学生的学习兴趣。

奥利和莫莉会引导学生进行思考、合作与交流。

设置问题，激活学生的背景知识，引导学生进行思辨。

听前准备和听力训练

学生学习重点词汇，并在本书后面的“图解词典”中写出相应的单词或短语。

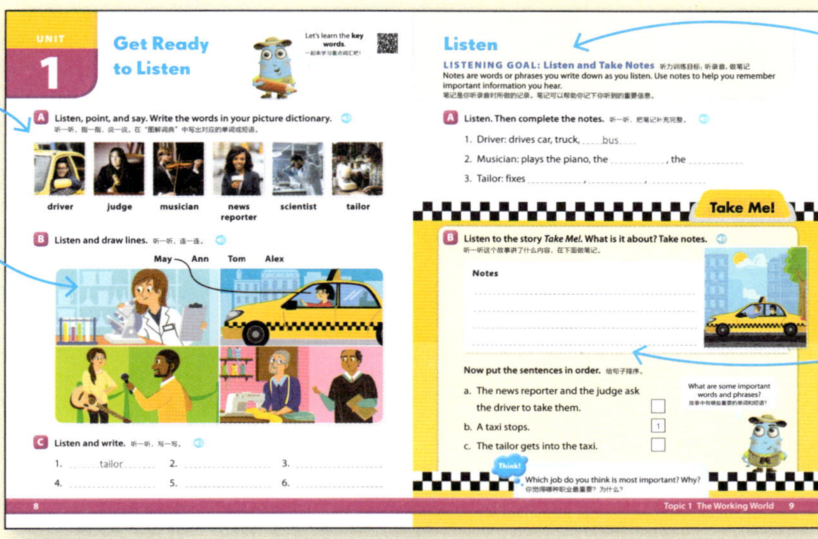

这里介绍了超级实用的听力学习策略。

听力学习策略能帮助学生应对不同类型的听力材料，不管是虚构类的还是非虚构类的。听录音的时候，学生应联系生活实际进行思辨。

* 每个话题包含两个主题相近的单元。

加深理解

引导学生运用听力学习策略来更好地理解听到的内容。

设置相关练习，帮助学生进一步掌握所学词汇。

Understand

A Think about *Take Me!*. Which note has important information?
回想一下故事。下列哪条笔记中包含重要信息？
a. Tailor: fixes clothes for people
b. Tailor: smiles

Remember! Take notes about important information.

B Listen to *Take Me!* again. Choose the correct answer.
再听一听故事，圈出正确的答案。
1. Four / Seven people run to the taxi.
2. The first person to speak is the judge / tailor.
3. The tailor says his job is the most interesting / most important.
4. The musicians and the scientists / judge and the news reporter leave.
5. The driver takes the scientist / tailor.

C Listen. Complete each sentence with a key word. Then match.
1. The judge works in a court.
2. The ______ can drive a taxi.
3. The ______ talks to people.
4. The ______ has an important job.
a. 1 b. c. d.

10

D Listen to *Take Me!* again. Work with a partner. Complete the diagram.
再听一听故事，和小伙伴一起完成思维导图。
One Person: 1. judge 2. 3. 4.
Two or More People: 5. 6.

E Look at D. Complete the sentences. Use *is* or *are*.
回顾上一题，用is或are完成句子。
1. He is a judge.
2. They
3. She
4. They

MY LISTENING GOALS
I can listen to the story.
I can take notes to remember important information.

Topic 1 The Working World 11

检验学生对本单元内容，包括词汇和语法的掌握程度。

设置更多练习，帮助学生了解不同的题型，以更好地应对考试。

听力测试

奥利和莉莉会引导学生运用学到的听力学习策略。

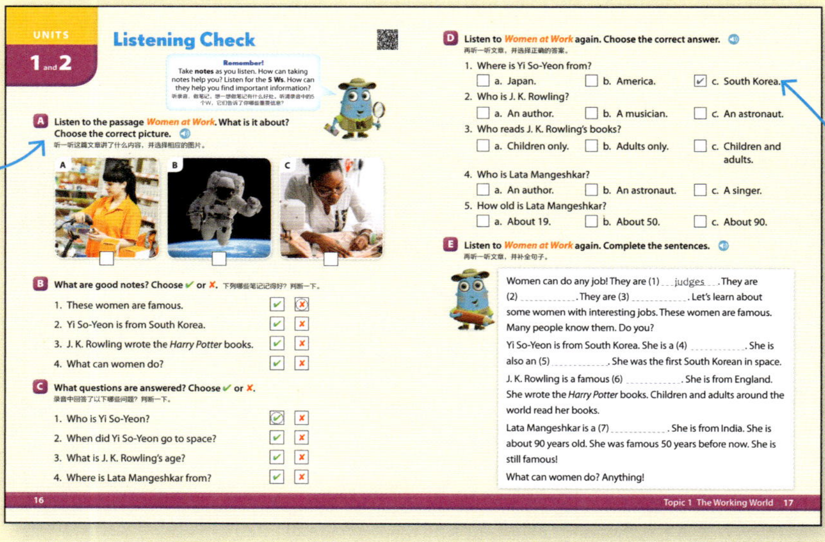
UNITS 1 and 2

Listening Check

Remember! Take notes as you listen. How can taking notes help you? Listen for the 5 Ws. How can they help you find important information?

A Listen to the passage *Women at Work*. What is it about? Choose the correct picture.
A B C

B What are good notes? Choose ✓ or ✗.
1. These women are famous.
2. Yi So-Yeon is from South Korea.
3. J. K. Rowling wrote the *Harry Potter* books.
4. What can women do?

C What questions are answered? Choose ✓ or ✗.
1. Who is Yi So-Yeon?
2. When did Yi So-Yeon go to space?
3. What is J. K. Rowling's age?
4. Where is Lata Mangeshkar from?

16

D Listen to *Women at Work* again. Choose the correct answer.
1. Where is Yi So-Yeon from? a. Japan. b. America. c. South Korea.
2. Who is J. K. Rowling? a. An author. b. A musician. c. An astronaut.
3. Who reads J. K. Rowling's books? a. Children only. b. Adults only. c. Children and adults.
4. Who is Lata Mangeshkar? a. An author. b. An astronaut. c. A singer.
5. How old is Lata Mangeshkar? a. About 19. b. About 50. c. About 90.

E Listen to *Women at Work* again. Complete the sentences.
Women can do any job! They are (1) judges. They are (2) ______. They are (3) ______. Let's learn about some women with interesting jobs. These women are famous. Many people know them. Do you?
Yi So-Yeon is from South Korea. She is a (4) ______. She is also an (5) ______. She was the first South Korean in space.
J. K. Rowling is a famous (6) ______. She is from England. She wrote the *Harry Potter* books. Children and adults around the world read her books.
Lata Mangeshkar is a (7) ______. She is from India. She is about 90 years old. She was famous 50 years before now. She is still famous!
What can women do? Anything!

Topic 1 The Working World 17

学生完成相关练习，进一步强化听力理解和词汇运用能力。

口语交际和说一说

口语训练目标
旨在帮助学生在不同的场景下自信表达。

口语练习小贴士
提供语法、标点符号和学习策略方面的指导，帮助学生准确、流利地交流。

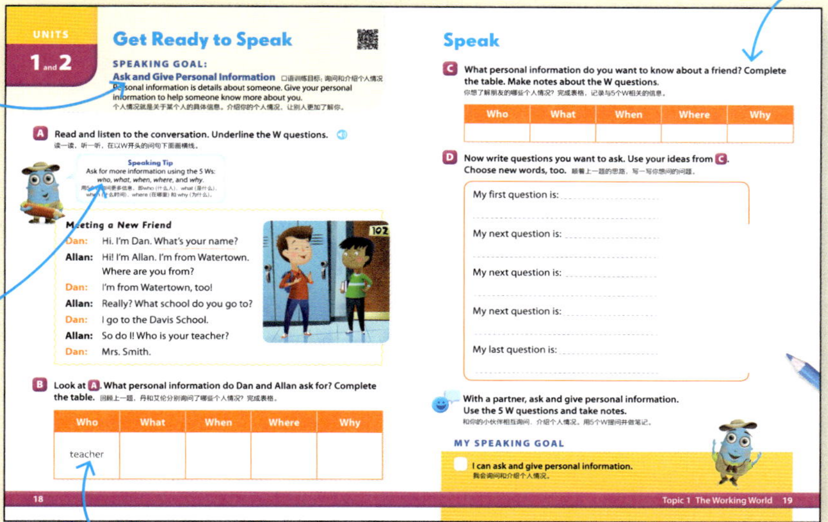
UNITS 1 and 2

Get Ready to Speak

SPEAKING GOAL:
Ask and Give Personal Information
Personal information is details about someone. Give your personal information to help someone know more about you.

A Read and listen to the conversation. Underline the W questions.

Speaking Tip
Ask for more information using the 5 Ws: who, what, when, where, and why.

Meeting a New Friend
Dan: Hi. I'm Dan. What's your name?
Allan: Hi! I'm Allan. I'm from Watertown. Where are you from?
Dan: I'm from Watertown, too!
Allan: Really? What school do you go to?
Dan: I go to the Davis School.
Allan: So do I! Who is your teacher?
Dan: Mrs. Smith.

B Look at A. What personal information do Dan and Allan ask for? Complete the table.

Who	What	When	Where	Why
teacher				

Speak

C What personal information do you want to know about a friend? Complete the table. Make notes about the W questions.

Who	What	When	Where	Why

D Now write questions you want to ask. Use your ideas from C. Choose new words, too.

My first question is: ____________
My next question is: ____________
My next question is: ____________
My next question is: ____________
My last question is: ____________

With a partner, ask and give personal information. Use the 5 W questions and take notes.

MY SPEAKING GOAL
I can ask and give personal information.

18 Topic 1 The Working World 19

提供"脚手架式"口语交际模板，帮助学生达成口语训练目标。

以思维导图的形式展示口语交际模板，帮助学生梳理思路。

练习册

设置形式多样的练习，帮助学生进一步运用所学的听力学习策略，提高听力理解能力。

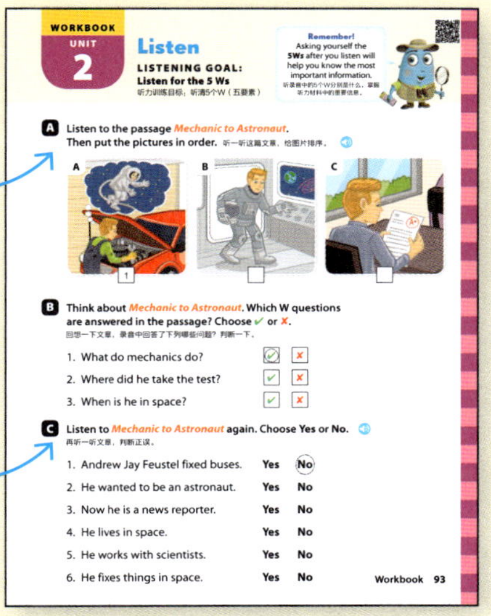
WORKBOOK UNIT 2

Listen

LISTENING GOAL:
Listen for the 5 Ws

Remember! Asking yourself the 5Ws after you listen will help you know the most important information.

A Listen to the passage *Mechanic to Astronaut*. Then put the pictures in order.

B Think about *Mechanic to Astronaut*. Which W questions are answered in the passage? Choose ✓ or ✗.

1. What do mechanics do?
2. Where did he take the test?
3. When is he in space?

C Listen to *Mechanic to Astronaut* again. Choose Yes or No.

1. Andrew Jay Feustel fixed buses. Yes No
2. He wanted to be an astronaut. Yes No
3. Now he is a news reporter. Yes No
4. He lives in space. Yes No
5. He works with scientists. Yes No
6. He fixes things in space. Yes No

Workbook 93

设置丰富的词汇练习，帮助学生提高听力理解和词汇运用能力。

引导学生在交流中使用规范、通顺的语言。

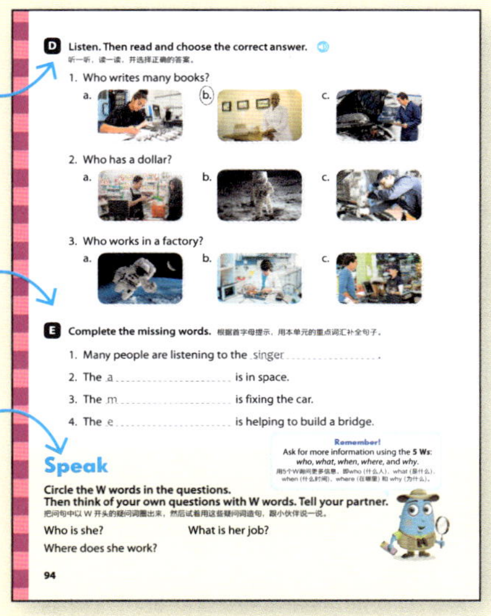
D Listen. Then read and choose the correct answer.

1. Who writes many books?
2. Who has a dollar?
3. Who works in a factory?

E Complete the missing words.

1. Many people are listening to the singer.
2. The a________ is in space.
3. The m________ is fixing the car.
4. The e________ is helping to build a bridge.

Speak

Remember! Ask for more information using the 5 Ws: who, what, when, where, and why.

Circle the W words in the questions. Then think of your own questions with W words. Tell your partner.

Who is she? What is her job?
Where does she work?

94

TOPIC 1

SCIENCE

The Working World

MY GOALS

UNIT 1

- Listen to the story *Take Me!*
- Listen and take notes

UNIT 2

- Listen to the passage *What Job Do You Want?*
- Listen for the 5 Ws

SPEAK

- Ask and give personal information

A **Look at the picture. What do you see?**
看图片，回答问题。

1. Where are the people?
   What are they doing?
2. Where do you want to work one day?
   Why?

FUN FACT

Listen

Time at Work

B **Listen to the Fun Fact. Then answer the questions.** 听“奇闻趣事”，回答问题。

1. How many hours do most people work every day?
2. Is that a lot of time to work? Why or why not?

Think, Pair, Share
What jobs are interesting? Why?
什么工作很有意思？为什么？

UNIT

1 Get Ready to Listen

Let's learn the **key words**.
一起来学习重点词汇吧！

A Listen, point, and say. Write the words in your picture dictionary.

听一听，指一指，说一说。在“图解词典”中写出对应的单词或短语。

driver

judge

musician

news reporter

scientist

tailor

B Listen and draw lines. 听一听，连一连。

May Ann Tom Alex

C Listen and write. 听一听，写一写。

1. tailor
2. ______
3. ______
4. ______
5. ______
6. ______

Listen

LISTENING GOAL: Listen and Take Notes 听力训练目标：听录音，做笔记

Notes are words or phrases you write down as you listen. Use notes to help you remember important information you hear.

笔记是你听录音时所做的记录。笔记可以帮助你记下你听到的重要信息。

A **Listen. Then complete the notes.** 听一听，把笔记补充完整。

1. Driver: drives car, truck, ___bus___
2. Musician: plays the piano, the __________, the __________
3. Tailor: fixes __________, __________, __________

Take Me!

B **Listen to the story *Take Me!*. What is it about? Take notes.**

听一听这个故事讲了什么内容，在下面做笔记。

Notes

____

____

____

____

Now put the sentences in order. 给句子排序。

a. The news reporter and the judge ask the driver to take them. ☐

b. A taxi stops. 1

c. The tailor gets into the taxi. ☐

What are some important words and phrases?

故事中有哪些重要的单词和短语？

Think!

Which job do you think is most important? Why?

你觉得哪种职业最重要？为什么？

Understand

A **Think about *Take Me!*. Which note has important information?**

回想一下故事，下列哪条笔记中包含重要信息？

- [ ] a. Tailor: fixes clothes for people
- [ ] b. Tailor: smiles

Remember!
Take **notes** about important information.
把重要信息记下来。

B **Listen to *Take Me!* again. Choose the correct answer.**

再听一听故事，圈出正确的答案。

1. **Four** / **Seven** people run to the taxi. (Seven circled)
2. The first person to speak is the **judge** / **tailor**.
3. The tailor says his job is the **most interesting** / **most important**.
4. The **musicians and the scientists** / **judge and the news reporter** leave.
5. The driver takes the **scientist** / **tailor**.

C **Listen. Complete each sentence with a key word. Then match.**

听一听，用本单元的重点词汇补全句子，并与相应的图片配对。

1. The ______ judge ______ works in a court.
2. The ____________ can drive a taxi.
3. The ____________ talks to people.
4. The ____________ has an important job.

a. __1__

b. ____

c. ____

d. ____

D Listen to *Take Me!* again. Work with a partner. Complete the diagram.

再听一听故事，和小伙伴一起完成思维导图。

One Person

1. judge
2. ____________
3. ____________
4. ____________

Two or More People

5. ____________
6. ____________

E Look at D. Complete the sentences. Use *is* or *are*.

回顾上一题，用is或are完成句子。

1. 

He ______ is a judge ______.

2. 

They ____________________.

3. 

She ____________________.

4. 

They ____________________.

MY LISTENING GOALS

- [ ] I can listen to the story. 我能听懂这个故事。
- [ ] I can take notes to remember important information. 我会做笔记，记下重要信息。

UNIT

2 Get Ready to Listen

Let's learn the **key words.**
一起来学习重点词汇吧！

A Listen, point, and say. Write the words in your picture dictionary.

听一听，指一指，说一说。在“图解词典”中写出对应的单词。

astronaut

author

cashier

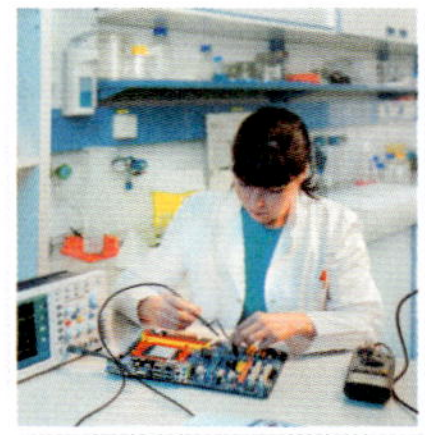

engineer

mechanic

singer

B Listen and number. 听一听，在圆圈里填上正确的序号。

C Listen and complete the sentences. 听一听，并补全句子。

1. The ___cashier___ works eight hours every day.
2. The ________ and the ________ are fixing the problem together.
3. The ________ has an exciting job.
4. The ________ and the ________ are friends.

Listen

LISTENING GOAL: Listen for the 5 Ws 听力训练目标：听清5个W（五要素）

The 5 Ws are *who, what, when, where,* and *why*. After you listen, ask yourself the 5 Ws to know the most important information. 5个W分别为who（什么人）、what（是什么）、when（什么时间）、where（在哪里）和why（为什么）。仔细听录音中的5个W分别是什么，掌握听力材料中的重要信息。

A Listen. What does the sentence tell you?

听一听，下列句子传递了什么信息？

1. ☐ a. why ☑ b. where
2. ☐ a. what ☐ b. when
3. ☐ a. when ☐ b. where

What Job Do You Want?

B Listen to the passage *What Job Do You Want?*. What is it about? Choose the correct picture.

听一听这篇文章讲了什么内容，并选择相应的图片。

A

☐

B

☐

Now choose ✔ or ✘. 判断正误。

1. The people are talking in a classroom. ☑ ✔ ☐ ✘
2. The people are talking about their jobs. ☐ ✔ ☐ ✘
3. One person is a cashier. ☐ ✔ ☐ ✘

What information do you learn about each job?
关于每一种职业，你都了解了哪些信息？

Think!

Which job is interesting to you? Why?
你觉得哪种职业很有趣？为什么？

Understand

Remember!
When you listen, the **5 Ws** (*who*, *what*, *when*, *where*, *why*) help you know the most important information.
听录音时，5个W ——who (什么人)、what (是什么)、when (什么时间)、where (在哪里) 和 why (为什么) 能帮助你掌握重要信息。

A **Think about *What Job Do You Want?*. Did you hear the answers to these questions? Choose Yes or No.**
回想一下，你是否在文章中听到了下列问题的答案？判断一下。

1. What does an engineer do? **Yes** **No**
2. Where do authors work? **Yes** **No**

B **Listen to *What Job Do You Want?* again. Choose the correct answer.**
再听一听文章，选择正确的答案。

1. Where do mechanics work?
   ☑ a. In garages. ☐ b. In schools.
2. Who is an engineer?
   ☐ a. Bill. ☐ b. Jan.
3. What is Ellen's job?
   ☐ a. She's an engineer. ☐ b. She's an astronaut.

C **Listen and choose the correct picture. Then write the key word.**
听一听，选择恰当的图片，并将相应的词写在下方的横线上。

1.

☑ a

☐ b

engineer

2.

☐ a

☐ b

____

3.

☐ a

☐ b

____

4.

☐ a

☐ b

____

D Listen to ***What Job Do You Want?*** again. Work with a partner. Complete the table. 再听一听文章，和小伙伴一起完成表格。

What do …	What does …
1. mechanics	2.
3.	4.

E Look at **D**. Write. Ask about the job. Use *What* + *do* or *does*.
回顾上一题，用What do或What does写一写关于职业的问句。

1.

What do mechanics do?

2.

3.

4.

MY LISTENING GOALS

- ☐ I can listen to the passage. 我能听懂这篇文章。
- ☐ I can listen for the 5 Ws to find important information.
我能听清录音中的5个W，掌握文章中的重要信息。

UNITS
1 and 2

Listening Check

Remember!
Take **notes** as you listen. How can taking notes help you? Listen for the **5 Ws**. How can they help you find important information?
听录音，做笔记。想一想做笔记有什么好处。听清录音中的5个W，它们告诉了你哪些重要信息？

A Listen to the passage *Women at Work*. What is it about? Choose the correct picture.
听一听这篇文章讲了什么内容，并选择相应的图片。

A

☐

B

☐

C
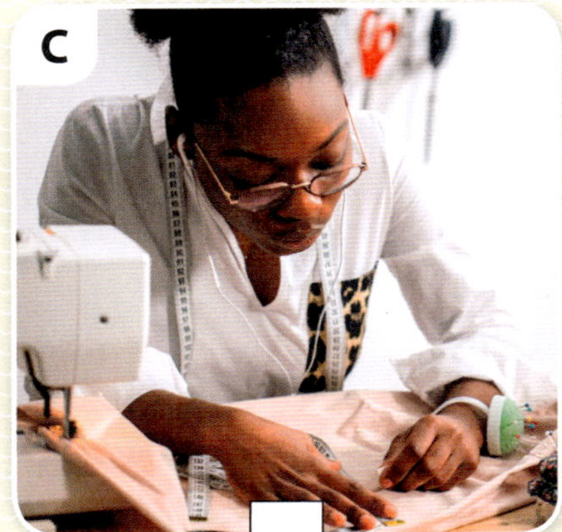
☐

B What are good notes? Choose ✔ or ✘. 下列哪些笔记记得好？判断一下。

1. These women are famous. ✔ (✘)
2. Yi So-Yeon is from South Korea. ✔ ✘
3. J. K. Rowling wrote the *Harry Potter* books. ✔ ✘
4. What can women do? ✔ ✘

C What questions are answered? Choose ✔ or ✘.
录音中回答了以下哪些问题？判断一下。

1. Who is Yi So-Yeon? (✔) ✘
2. When did Yi So-Yeon go to space? ✔ ✘
3. What is J. K. Rowling's age? ✔ ✘
4. Where is Lata Mangeshkar from? ✔ ✘

D Listen to *Women at Work* again. Choose the correct answer.

再听一听文章，并选择正确的答案。

1. Where is Yi So-Yeon from?

   ☐ a. Japan. ☐ b. America. ☑ c. South Korea.

2. Who is J. K. Rowling?

   ☐ a. An author. ☐ b. A musician. ☐ c. An astronaut.

3. Who reads J. K. Rowling's books?

   ☐ a. Children only. ☐ b. Adults only. ☐ c. Children and adults.

4. Who is Lata Mangeshkar?

   ☐ a. An author. ☐ b. An astronaut. ☐ c. A singer.

5. How old is Lata Mangeshkar?

   ☐ a. About 19. ☐ b. About 50. ☐ c. About 90.

E Listen to *Women at Work* again. Complete the sentences.

再听一听文章，并补全句子。

Women can do any job! They are (1) judges. They are (2) ________. They are (3) ________. Let's learn about some women with interesting jobs. These women are famous. Many people know them. Do you?

Yi So-Yeon is from South Korea. She is a (4) ________. She is also an (5) ________. She was the first South Korean in space.

J. K. Rowling is a famous (6) ________. She is from England. She wrote the *Harry Potter* books. Children and adults around the world read her books.

Lata Mangeshkar is a (7) ________. She is from India. She is about 90 years old. She was famous 50 years before now. She is still famous!

What can women do? Anything!

UNITS 1 and 2

Get Ready to Speak

SPEAKING GOAL:

Ask and Give Personal Information 口语训练目标：询问和介绍个人情况

Personal information is details about someone. Give your personal information to help someone know more about you.

个人情况就是关于某个人的具体信息。介绍你的个人情况，让别人更加了解你。

A **Read and listen to the conversation. Underline the W questions.**

读一读，听一听，在以W开头的问句下面画横线。

Speaking Tip

Ask for more information using the 5 Ws: *who*, *what*, *when*, *where*, and *why*.

用5个W询问更多信息，即who (什么人)、what (是什么)、when (什么时间)、where (在哪里) 和 why (为什么)。

Meeting a New Friend

Dan: Hi. I'm Dan. What's your name?

Allan: Hi! I'm Allan. I'm from Watertown. Where are you from?

Dan: I'm from Watertown, too!

Allan: Really? What school do you go to?

Dan: I go to the Davis School.

Allan: So do I! Who is your teacher?

Dan: Mrs. Smith.

B **Look at A. What personal information do Dan and Allan ask for? Complete the table.** 回顾上一题，丹和艾伦分别询问了哪些个人情况？完成表格。

Who	What	When	Where	Why
teacher				

Speak

C **What personal information do you want to know about a friend? Complete the table. Make notes about the W questions.**
你想了解朋友的哪些个人情况？完成表格，记录与5个W相关的信息。

Who	What	When	Where	Why

D **Now write questions you want to ask. Use your ideas from C. Choose new words, too.** 顺着上一题的思路，写一写你想问的问题。

My first question is: ____________________

____

My next question is: ____________________

____

My next question is: ____________________

____

My next question is: ____________________

____

My last question is: ____________________

____

With a partner, ask and give personal information. Use the 5 W questions and take notes.
和你的小伙伴相互询问、介绍个人情况。用5个W提问并做笔记。

MY SPEAKING GOAL

☐ **I can ask and give personal information.**
我会询问和介绍个人情况。

TOPIC

2

MATH

In My Backpack

MY GOALS

UNIT 3

- Listen to the passage *The First Day of School*
- Listen for facts

UNIT 4

- Listen to the story *Tim's Tablet*
- Listen for opinions

SPEAK

- Agree and disagree

A **Look at the picture. What do you see?**
看图片，回答问题。

1. What are the children doing?
   What are they using?
2. What do you use in your classroom?

FUN FACT

Listen

Computers and Classrooms

B **Listen to the Fun Fact. Then answer the questions.** 听“奇闻趣事”，回答问题。

1. How many books can a tablet have?
2. Do you like using tablets? Why or why not?

Think, Pair, Share
In your classroom, what helps you learn?
在课堂上，哪些东西能帮助你学习？

UNIT

3

Get Ready to Listen

A Listen, point, and say. Write the words in your picture dictionary.

听一听，指一指，说一说。在“图解词典”中写出对应的单词。

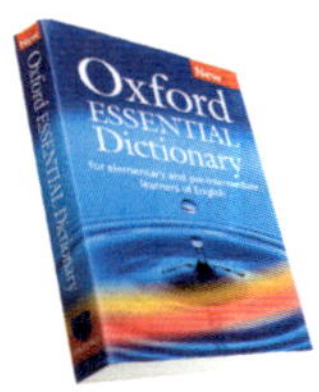

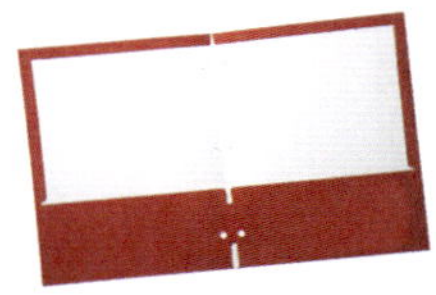

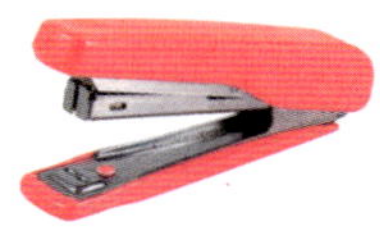

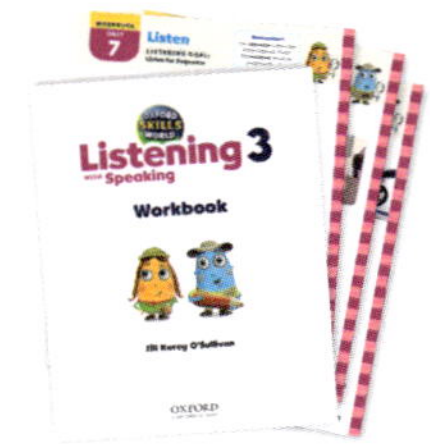

calculator dictionary folder scissors stapler workbook

B Listen and draw lines. 听一听，连一连。

Milo Anita Ella Ben

C Listen and write. 听一听，写一写。

1. ____________ 2. ____________ 3. ____________

4. ____________ 5. ____________ 6. ____________

Listen

LISTENING GOAL: Listen for Facts 听力训练目标：明确事实

A fact is something that is true for everyone. For example, *The workbook is blue* is a fact. Listen for facts to know what is true in a listening. 事实就是真实情况，对每个人来说都是如此。例如，“这本练习册是蓝色的”就是事实。听录音，明确哪些是事实。

A **Listen. Is the sentence a fact? Complete the sentences with *is* or *is not*.**
听一听，下列句子是事实吗？用is或is not补全句子。

1. This ________ a fact.
2. This ________ a fact.
3. This ________ a fact.

The First Day of School

B **Listen to the passage *The First Day of School*. What is it about? Choose the correct picture.**
听一听这篇文章讲了什么内容，并选择相应的图片。

A

B

Now put the sentences in order. 给句子排序。

a. The teacher sees that Asha and Abdul are smiling. ☐
b. The teacher says, “Please bring your calculator.” ☐
c. The teacher welcomes the students. ☐

What **facts** do you hear in the listening?
你从录音中听到了哪些事实？

Think!
What do you bring to school every day?
你每天都带什么去学校？

Understand

A Think about ***The First Day of School***. What fact did you hear?

回想一下文章，你听到了哪些事实？

☐ a. The classroom has scissors.

☐ b. Smiles are great!

Remember!
Facts are true for everyone.
事实就是真实情况，对每个人来说都是如此。

B Listen to ***The First Day of School*** again. Choose the correct answer.

再听一听文章，圈出正确的答案。

1. The teacher's name is Mrs. **White** / **Black**.
2. The classroom has a **dictionary** / **calculator** for each student to use.
3. Students need to bring their folder **every day** / **on Monday**.
4. Every day, students need to bring **three** / **four** things.
5. Asha is **smiling** / **crying**.

C Listen. Complete each sentence with a key word. Then match.

听一听，用本单元的重点词汇补全句子，并与相应的图片配对。

1. Can you please give me the ________?
2. I have a ________ in my desk.
3. The ________ is on the desk.
4. My teacher gave me a ________ to use.

a. ____ 

b. ____ 

c. ____ 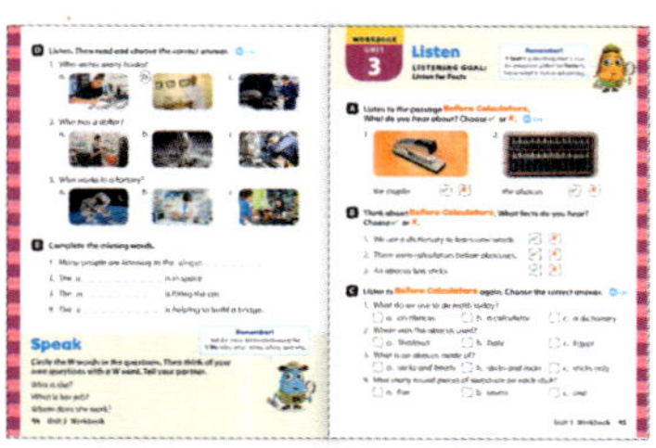

d. ____ 

D Listen to *The First Day of School* again. Who has the things? Work with a partner. Complete the table.

再听一听文章，谁有下列物品？和小伙伴一起完成表格。

	teacher	classroom	students	Asha and Abdul
1. dictionaries				
2. calculators				
3. workbooks	✔			
4. smiles				

E Look at D. Complete the sentences with *has* or *have* and the things.

回顾上一题，用has或have完成句子。

1. 

The teacher has workbooks.

2. 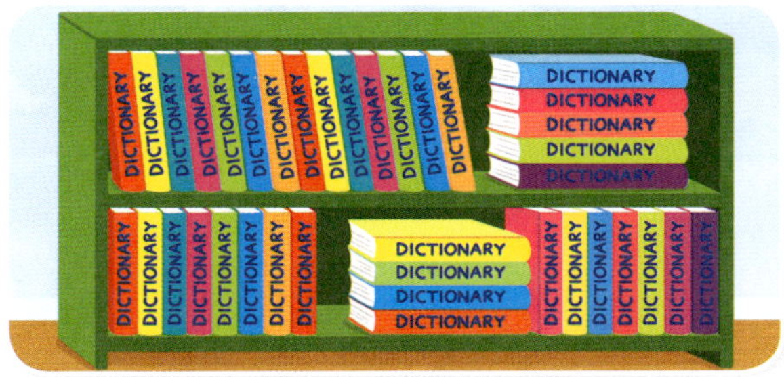

The classroom ______________.

3. 

The students ______________
______________.

4. 

Asha and Abdul ______________
______________.

MY LISTENING GOALS

- ☐ **I can listen to the passage.** 我能听懂这篇文章。
- ☐ **I can listen for facts to know what is true in a listening.**
  我能搞清楚录音中哪些内容是事实。

UNIT 4

Get Ready to Listen

Let's learn the **key words**.
一起来学习重点词汇吧！

A **Listen, point, and say. Write the words in your picture dictionary.**
听一听，指一指，说一说。在“图解词典”中写出对应的单词。

cabinet

drawer

flag

laptop

shelf

tablet

B **Listen and number.** 听一听，在圆圈里填上正确的序号。

C **Listen and complete the sentences.** 听一听，并补全句子。

1. There is a ____________ in every classroom.
2. The student is using the ____________.
3. The scissors are on the ____________ or in the ____________.
4. The boy put his ____________ in the ____________.

Listen

LISTENING GOAL: Listen for Opinions 听力训练目标：明确观点

An opinion is what a person thinks about something. It is not true for everyone. For example, *I think the activities in the workbook are difficult* is an opinion. Listen for opinions to know how people feel.

观点就是一个人对事物或问题的看法，每个人的观点不尽相同。例如，“我觉得练习册里面的题很难”就是观点。听录音，明确观点，了解人们的看法。

A **Listen. Is the sentence a fact or an opinion? Choose the correct answer.**

听一听，这些句子是在陈述事实还是在表达观点？选择正确的答案。

1. ☐ fact ☐ opinion
2. ☐ fact ☐ opinion
3. ☐ fact ☐ opinion

Tim's Tablet

B **Listen to the story *Tim's Tablet*. What is it about? Choose the correct picture.**

听一听这个故事讲了什么内容，并选择相应的图片。

A

☐

B

☐

Now choose ✔ or ✘. 判断正误。

1. Tim can't find his tablet. ✔ ✘
2. His classmates help him look for it. ✔ ✘
3. They find the tablet in a cabinet. ✔ ✘

Who says an **opinion**? What is it?
谁表达了观点？是什么观点？

Think!

How do you feel when you lose something? Why?
丢了东西时，你有什么感受？为什么？

Understand

Remember!
Listen for **opinions** to know how people feel.
明确观点，了解人们的看法。

A Think about *Tim's Tablet*. Are the sentences opinions? Choose Yes or No.

回想一下故事，下列句子表达的是观点吗？判断正误。

1. There are ten children. **Yes** **No**
2. She thinks he looks sad. **Yes** **No**

B Listen to *Tim's Tablet* again. Choose the correct answer.

再听一听故事，选择正确的答案。

1. Where does Tim look for his tablet?
   - ☐ a. In his drawer.
   - ☐ b. In his backpack.
2. How many children are there in the class?
   - ☐ a. Nine.
   - ☐ b. Ten.
3. Where is Tim's tablet?
   - ☐ a. On the teacher's desk.
   - ☐ b. At home.

C Listen and choose the correct picture. Then write the key word.

听一听，选择恰当的图片，并将相应的词写在下方的横线上。

1.

☐ a

☐ b

____

2.

☐ a

☐ b

____

3.

☐ a

☐ b

____

4.

☐ a

☐ b

____

D Listen to *Tim's Tablet* again. Work with a partner. Complete the diagram. 再听一听故事，和小伙伴一起完成思维导图。

~~he~~	the classmates	the teacher	they

What is

1. he
2. ______

What are

3. ______
4. ______

E Look at D. Write a question. Use *What* + *is* or *are*.

参照上一题，用What is或What are完成问句。

1. 

What is he looking for?

2. 

______ the teacher looking for?

3. 

______ they looking for?

4. 

______ the classmates looking for?

MY LISTENING GOALS

- ☐ **I can listen to the story.** 我能听懂这个故事。
- ☐ **I can listen for opinions to know how people feel.** 我能明确观点，了解人们的看法。

UNITS

3 and 4

Listening Check

Remember!
Listen for **facts**. What does a fact tell you? Listen for **opinions**. What does an opinion tell you?
明确事实，事实告诉了你什么？明确观点，观点告诉了你什么？

A Listen to the story ***Can I Use Your Dictionary?***.
What is it about? Choose the correct picture.
听一听这个故事讲了什么内容，并选择相应的图片。

A

☐

B

☐

C

☐

B Which facts are true? Choose ✔ or ✘.
下列哪些句子说的是事实？判断正误。

1. The teacher asks Sal and Cora to be partners. ✔ ✘
2. Sal has his dictionary in class today. ✔ ✘
3. Cora shares her workbook with Sal. ✔ ✘
4. There are no scissors in the cabinet. ✔ ✘

C Which sentences are opinions? Choose ✔ or ✘.
下列哪些句子表达的是观点？判断正误。

1. Sal asks for Cora's calculator. ✔ ✘
2. Sal thinks Cora is smart. ✔ ✘
3. Sal has everything at home. ✔ ✘
4. Cora thinks Sal is nice. ✔ ✘

D Listen to *Can I Use Your Dictionary?* again. Choose the correct answer.

再听一听故事，并选择正确的答案。

1. Who asks Sal and Cora to be partners?
   - ☐ a. Sal.
   - ☐ b. Cora.
   - ☐ c. The teacher.
2. Why is Sal happy to be Cora's partner?
   - ☐ a. She's his best friend.
   - ☐ b. She has a workbook.
   - ☐ c. She's smart.
3. What does Sal ask Cora for first?
   - ☐ a. Her calculator.
   - ☐ b. Her workbook.
   - ☐ c. Her dictionary.
4. What is in the cabinet?
   - ☐ a. Workbooks.
   - ☐ b. Scissors.
   - ☐ c. Dictionaries.
5. Where are Sal's things?
   - ☐ a. In class.
   - ☐ b. In his backpack.
   - ☐ c. At home.

E Listen to *Can I Use Your Dictionary?* again. Complete the sentences.

再听一听故事，并补全句子。

The teacher asks Sal and Cora to be partners.

Sal says, "I'm glad you're my partner, Cora. You're so smart."

Cora says, "Thanks, Sal. You're so nice!"

Sal asks, "Can I use your (1) ____________?" Cora says, "Sure!"

Then Sal asks, "Can I see your (2) ____________?" Cora says, "OK."

Soon, Sal says, "Can I look at your (3) ____________?"

Cora says, "OK. But don't ask for my (4) ____________ or my (5) ____________. There are some in the (6) ____________."

Sal says, "Thanks!"

Cora asks, "Why don't you have anything today?"

Sal says, "Oh. I do have everything." "You do?" asks Cora.

"Yes!" Sal says. "At home!"

UNITS 3 and 4

Get Ready to Speak

SPEAKING GOAL: Agree and Disagree

口语训练目标：表示赞同和反对

You agree with someone when you have the same opinion.
You disagree when you have a different opinion. 当你和别人的观点一致时，你就会赞同他的观点。当你和别人的观点不一致时，你就会反对他的观点。

A **Read and listen to the conversation. Underline the words that show Ana and Ned agree and disagree.**

读一读，听一听，在安娜和内德表示赞同和反对的句子下面画横线。

Speaking Tip

Use *you're right* to agree. Use *I don't think so* to disagree.
用you're right表示赞同，用I don't think so表示反对。

The Important Things

Ana: What are the important things we use in class? What do you think?

Ned: Calculators!

Ana: Really? Why?

Ned: They make math easier!

Ana: I don't think so. I don't think they are important. We can do math without them.

Ned: What do you think is important?

Ana: I think dictionaries are important.

Ned: You're right. Dictionaries are very important.

B **Look at A. What do Ana and Ned agree and disagree about? Complete the table.** 回顾上一题，安娜和内德赞同什么、反对什么？完成表格。

They agree about ...	They disagree about ...
1.	2.

Speak

C **Think about things in your classroom. Are they important or not? Complete the table with your opinion.**

想一想教室里有哪些东西，这些东西重要吗？根据你的观点完成表格。

Important	Not Important

D **Now write about your opinions. Use your ideas from C. Choose new words, too. Then draw the important things.**

顺着上一题的思路，写一写你的观点，并把你觉得重要的东西画出来。

I think ______________________________

____

____

I don't think ______________________________

____

____

With a partner, talk about things in the classroom. Are they important or not? Ask for your partner's opinions. Do you agree or disagree?

和小伙伴聊一聊教室里的东西有哪些是重要的，哪些是不重要的。小伙伴有什么观点？你同意他的观点吗？

MY SPEAKING GOAL

☐ **I can agree and disagree.**

我会表示赞同和反对。

TOPIC

3

SOCIAL STUDIES

I Like Your Clothes

MY GOALS

UNIT 5

- Listen to the conversation *Shopping with Mom*
- Listen for preferences

UNIT 6

- Listen to the story *The Little Brother*
- Listen for reasons

SPEAK

- Give preferences

A **Look at the picture. What do you see?**
看图片，回答问题。

1. Where are the girls? What are they doing?
2. Did you last shop for clothes online or in a store? What did you buy?

FUN FACT

Listen

Clothes Shopping

B **Listen to the Fun Fact. Then answer the questions.** 听“奇闻趣事”，回答问题。

1. Why do people like shopping for clothes in stores?
2. How do you usually shop?

Think, Pair, Share
Do you like shopping for clothes? Why or why not?
你喜欢买衣服吗？为什么？

UNIT

5

Get Ready to Listen

A Listen, point, and say. Write the words in your picture dictionary.

听一听，指一指，说一说。在“图解词典”中写出对应的单词。

baseball cap

coat

handbag

shorts

sneakers

swimsuit

B Listen and draw lines. 听一听，连一连。

Bess **Lisa** **Tom** **Jack**

C Listen and write. 听一听，写一写。

1. ________ 2. ________ 3. ________

4. ________ 5. ________ 6. ________

Listen

LISTENING GOAL: Listen for Preferences 听力训练目标：明确偏好

A preference is when you like one thing more than another thing.
Listen for *I prefer* and *I like* to know about preferences.
偏好就是相比之下，你更喜欢什么。注意听 I prefer 和 I like，它们常用于表达偏好。

A **Listen. Choose the correct answer.** 听一听，圈出正确的答案 。

1. Jan prefers the **orange handbag** / **pink handbag**.
2. Taro likes the **black coat** / **red coat** more.
3. Asha prefers to wear **shorts** / **pants**.

B **Listen to the conversation *Shopping with Mom*. What is it about? Choose the correct picture.**
听一听这段对话讲了什么内容，并选择相应的图片。

A

☐

B

☐

Now put the sentences in order. 给句子排序。

a. Mali's mom doesn't have enough money. ☐

b. Mali's mom says that the store has so many things. ☐

c. Mali says which shorts she likes. ☐

What does Mali say she likes? What does her mom prefer?
马利说她喜欢什么？她的妈妈更喜欢什么？

Think!

What kind of clothes do you like shopping for?
你喜欢买什么样的衣服？

Understand

A **Think about *Shopping with Mom*. What does Mali prefer?**
回想一下对话，马利更喜欢什么？

☐ a. The red shorts.
☐ b. The blue shorts.

Remember!
You can find **preferences** by listening for the words *I prefer* and *I like*.
注意听I prefer和I like等用于表达偏好的词。

B **Listen to *Shopping with Mom* again. Choose the correct answer.**
再听一听对话，圈出正确的答案。

1. Mali's mom says the store has everything from **coats to swimsuits** / **pants to baseball caps**.
2. Mali wants to buy a **baseball cap** / **handbag**.
3. Mali's mom shows Mali red **handbags** / **shorts**.
4. Mali's mom likes the **yellow** / **white** handbag.
5. Mali's mom doesn't have enough **time** / **money**.

C **Listen. Complete each sentence with a key word. Then match.**
听一听，用本单元的重点词汇补全句子，并与相应的图片配对。

1. I wear ________________ almost every day.
2. Bring your ________________ to the store.
3. Alec and I have the same ________________.
4. I like your ________________.

a. ____ 

b. ____ 

c. ____ 

d. ____ 

D Listen to ***Shopping with Mom*** again. Do Mali and her mom like the things? Work with a partner. Complete the table.

再听一听对话，马利和她的妈妈喜欢下列物品吗？和小伙伴一起完成表格。

Do you like the ...	Yes	No
1. red shorts		✔
2. blue shorts		
3. white handbag		
4. yellow handbag		

E Look at **D**. Complete the sentences. 回顾上一题，补全句子。

1. 

Mom: Do you like the red shorts?

Mali: ___No___, I ___don't___.

2. 

Mom: Do you like the blue shorts?

Mali: __________, I __________.

3. 

Mali: Do you like the white handbag?

Mom: __________, I __________.

4. 

Mali: Do you like the yellow handbag?

Mom: __________, I __________.

MY LISTENING GOALS

☐ **I can listen to the conversation.** 我能听懂这段对话。

☐ **I can listen for preferences.** 我能搞清楚人们的偏好。

UNIT

6

Get Ready to Listen

A Listen, point, and say. Write the words in your picture dictionary.

听一听，指一指，说一说。在"图解词典"中写出对应的单词。

clean

dirty

heavy

light

thick

thin

B Listen and number. 听一听，在圆圈里填上正确的序号。

C Listen and complete the sentences. 听一听，并补全句子。

1. The backpack is ____________.
2. The handbag is ____________.
3. Are the sneakers ____________ or ____________?
4. Your hair is ____________. It isn't ____________.

Listen

LISTENING GOAL: Listen for Reasons 听力训练目标：明确原因

A reason is why people do something or why something happens.
Listen for *because* to know reasons.
人们做某事的理由，或者某事发生的缘由，就是原因。注意听 because 来了解原因。

A Listen. Choose ✔ or ✘. 听一听，并判断正误。

1. 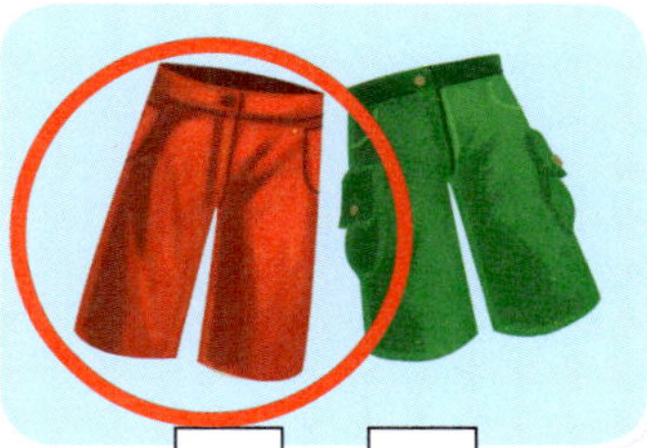
✔ ✘

2. 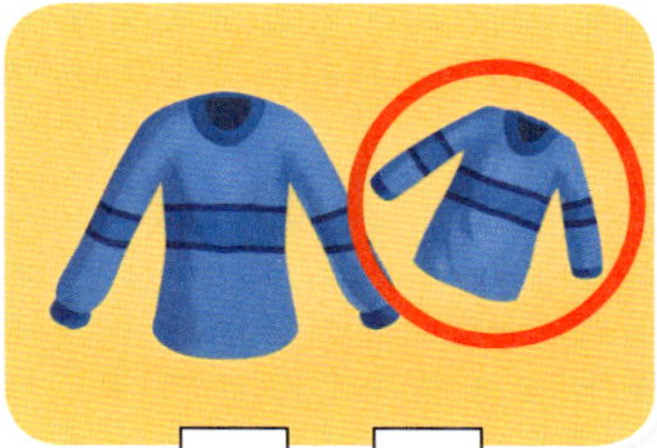
✔ ✘

3. 
✔ ✘

The Little Brother

B Listen to the story *The Little Brother*. What is it about? Choose the correct picture.
听一听这个故事讲了什么内容，并选择相应的图片。

A 

B 

Now choose ✔ or ✘. 判断正误。

1. Gil's shirt is dirty. ✔ ✘
2. The mother changes Gil's shirt. ✔ ✘
3. Gil doesn't like any of his shirts. ✔ ✘

What are some **reasons** in the story?
故事中提到了哪些原因？

Think!
What kind of clothes do you like to wear? Why?
你喜欢穿哪种衣服？为什么？

Understand

Remember!
Listen for the word *because* to find out **reasons**.
注意听because引导的句子，了解原因。

A **Think about *The Little Brother*. Do you hear a reason for each of these things? Choose Yes or No.**
回想一下故事，你听到下列事件的原因了吗？判断正误。

1. Why Gil needs a new shirt. **Yes** **No**
2. Why Marco likes Gil's shirt. **Yes** **No**

B **Listen to *The Little Brother* again. Choose the correct answer.**
再听一听故事，选择正确的答案。

1. What is Gil eating?
   ☐ a. A chocolate. ☐ b. A banana.
2. What color is Gil's shirt?
   ☐ a. Blue. ☐ b. Purple.
3. Why doesn't Gil like the purple shirt?
   ☐ a. It's too thick. ☐ b. It's too thin.

C **Listen and choose the correct picture. Then write the key word.**
听一听，选择恰当的图片，并将相应的词写在下方的横线上。

1.

☐ a

☐ b

____

2.

☐ a

☐ b

____

3.

☐ a

☐ b

____

4.

☐ a

☐ b

____

D Listen to ***The Little Brother*** again. What is the problem with each shirt? Work with a partner. Complete the diagram.

再听一听故事，每件衬衣各有什么问题？和小伙伴一起完成思维导图。

Shirt		Problem
1. blue shirt	→	too dirty
2. ______	→	______
3. ______	→	______
4. ______	→	______

E Look at **D**. Write the problem with each shirt. Use *too*.

回顾上一题，用too把每件衬衣的问题写出来。

1. 

The blue shirt is too dirty.

2. 

______

3. 

______

4. 

______

MY LISTENING GOALS

☐ I can listen to the story. 我能听懂这个故事。

☐ I can listen for a reason. 我能搞清楚原因。

UNITS 5 and 6

Listening Check

Remember!
Listen for **preferences**. What does someone *like* or *prefer*? Listen for **reasons**. What reason does someone give after the word *because*?
明确偏好，人们喜欢或更喜欢什么？明确原因，人们在because后面陈述了哪些理由？

A Listen to the article *What Clothes Do They Wear?*. What is it about? Choose the correct picture.

听一听这篇文章讲了什么内容，并选择相应的图片。

A
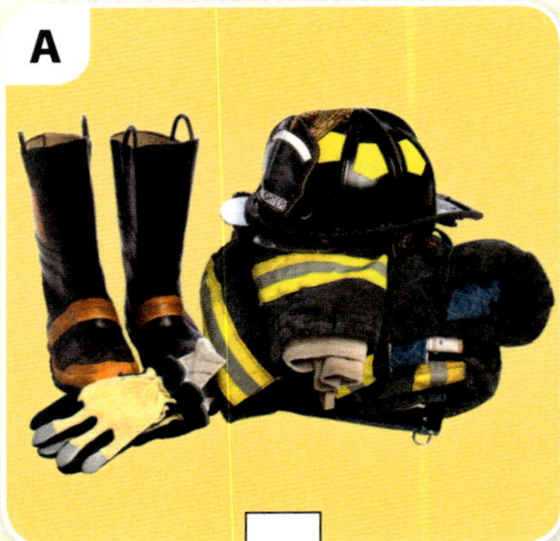
☐

B
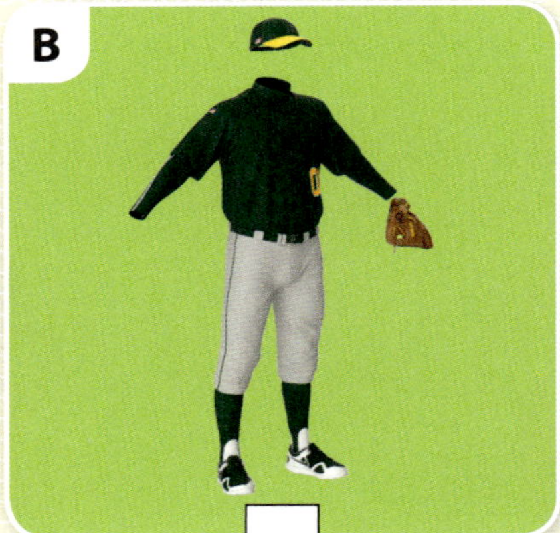
☐

C

☐

B What do baseball players prefer? Choose ✔ or ✘.

棒球运动员更喜欢穿什么？判断正误。

1. Shorts. ✔ ✘
2. Special pants. ✔ ✘
3. Cleats. ✔ ✘
4. Heavy clothes. ✔ ✘

C Why do baseball players wear special clothes? Choose ✔ or ✘.

为什么棒球运动员要穿特定的衣服？判断正误。

1. Because they are heavy. ✔ ✘
2. Because they are light. ✔ ✘
3. Because they are easy to run in. ✔ ✘
4. Because they are warm. ✔ ✘

D Listen to *What Clothes Do They Wear?* again. Choose the correct answer.

再听一听文章，并选择正确的答案。

1. Why do baseball players wear special clothes?

   ☐ a. To get dirty. ☐ b. To play well. ☐ c. To look good.

2. What are baseball sneakers called?

   ☐ a. Boots. ☐ b. Cleats. ☐ c. Shoes.

3. Why do baseball players wear cleats?

   ☐ a. To look good. ☐ b. To hit the ball. ☐ c. To help them run.

4. Baseball clothes are ____________.

   ☐ a. light ☐ b. heavy ☐ c. blue

5. What don't baseball players wear?

   ☐ a. A shirt. ☐ b. Pants. ☐ c. Shorts.

E Listen to *What Clothes Do They Wear?* again. Complete the sentences.

再听一听文章，并补全句子。

Baseball players wear special hats, shoes, and clothes. The players wear these things because they help them play well.

They wear (1) ____________ because these hats keep the sun out of their eyes. They wear special kinds of (2) ____________ called cleats. They prefer cleats because cleats help them run. They also help them not fall down. Players wear special pants and a shirt. These clothes are not (3) ____________. They are very (4) ____________. This helps them play and run. Baseball players do not wear (5) ____________. Why not? Because their legs get very (6) ____________ when they play!

Get Ready to Speak

SPEAKING GOAL: Give Preferences 口语训练目标：表达偏好

A preference is liking one thing more than another thing.
Give preferences to tell what you like.
偏好就是相比之下，更喜欢某样东西。表达偏好能让别人知道你喜欢什么。

A **Read and listen to the conversation. Underline the words for giving preferences.**
读一读，听一听，在表达偏好的词下面画横线。

Speaking Tip
Use the words *I prefer* and *I like* with *because* to give preferences.
用I prefer和 I like表达偏好，用because说明理由。

Ava: I want new sneakers. I want to ask my mom to take me shopping.

Pablo: You can ask her to buy you sneakers online.

Ava: I don't really like shopping on the computer.

Pablo: Why not?

Ava: I prefer to shop in stores.

Pablo: Really? Why?

Ava: Because I like to see things before I buy them. And I like going shopping. Which do you prefer?

Pablo: I'm not sure. I think I like shopping online because it's easy and fast!

Ava: That's true!

B **Look at A. What do they prefer? Why? Complete the table.**
回顾上一题，他们更喜欢什么？为什么？完成表格。

	Shop in store or online?	Why?
1. Pablo	online	
2. Ava		

Speak

C **Think about how or where you prefer to shop. Complete the table.**
想一想你更喜欢哪种购物方式？完成表格。

	Shop in store or online?	Why?
You		

D **Now write about how or where you like to shop and why. Use your ideas from C. Choose new words, too. Then draw something you want to buy.**
顺着上一题的思路，写一写你喜欢的购物方式，并把你想买的东西画出来。

I want ______________________________

I prefer ______________________________

____

because ______________________________

____

I also prefer ______________________________

____

because ______________________________

____

Work with a partner. Tell each other about how or where you like to shop.
和小伙伴互相讲一讲各自喜欢的购物方式。

MY SPEAKING GOAL

☐ **I can give preferences.**
我会表达偏好。

TOPIC

4 All Around Town

GEOGRAPHY

MY GOALS

UNIT 7

- Listen to the story *Fun Trip*
- Listen for sequence

UNIT 8

- Listen to the phone message *Come Over!*
- Listen for directions

SPEAK

- Ask for and give directions

A **Look at the picture. What do you see?**

看图片，回答问题。

1. Where are the people? What are they doing?
2. Name a place you were at with many people. Why were you there?

FUN FACT

Listen

City Life

B **Listen to the Fun Fact. Then answer the questions.** 听“奇闻趣事”，回答问题。

1. How many people live in Tokyo?
2. What is the special job in Tokyo? Is it fun? Why or why not?

Think, Pair, Share

Do you prefer to live in the city or the country? Why?

你更喜欢住在城市还是乡村？为什么？

UNIT

7

Get Ready to Listen

Let's learn the **key words.**
一起来学习重点词汇吧！

A Listen, point, and say. Write the words in your picture dictionary.
听一听，指一指，说一说。在“图解词典”中写出对应的单词

airport

bank

home

playground

post office

zoo

B Listen and draw lines. 听一听，连一连。

Jen **Prow** **Eva** **Dan** **Ms. Gomez** **Mr. Awad**

C Listen and write. 听一听，写一写。

1. ____________ 2. ____________ 3. ____________

4. ____________ 5. ____________ 6. ____________

Listen

LISTENING GOAL: Listen for Sequence 听力训练目标：理清顺序

The sequence is the order things happen. Listen for phrases like *to start*, *before*, and *after* to understand the sequence.
顺序就是事情发生的先后次序。注意听 to start、before 和 after 等词，它们常用于表示顺序。

A **Listen. Then complete the sentences.** 听一听，并补全句子。

1. To start, Adam's family has ____________.
2. Before Lin goes to the playground, she goes to ____________.
3. Jack visited his grandmother after he visited the ____________.

Fun Trip

B **Listen to the story *Fun Trip*. What is it about? Choose the correct picture.**
听一听这个故事讲了什么内容，并选择相应的图片。

A

☐

B

☐

Now put the sentences in order. 给句子排序。

a. Hanna doesn't want to leave. ☐
b. Hanna and Rosa go to the zoo. ☐
c. Rosa and her family meet Hanna at the airport. ☐

In what order do things happen in the story?
故事中的事情是按照什么顺序发生的？

Think!
Do you like to travel to new places? Why or why not?
你喜欢去没去过的地方旅行吗？为什么？

Understand

A **Think about *Fun Trip*. What is the first thing Hanna and Rosa do together?**

回想一下故事，汉娜和罗莎一起做的第一件事情是什么？

☐ a. They go to the playground.

☐ b. They go to the post office.

Remember!
Listen for **sequence** words like *to start*, *before*, and *after* to tell you the order things happen.
注意听to start、before和after等用于表示顺序的词。

B **Listen to *Fun Trip* again. Choose the correct answer.**

再听一听故事，圈出正确的答案。

1. Hanna and Rosa live in **the same** / **different** countries.
2. At first, Hanna feels **sad** / **happy**.
3. On Hanna's first day, they **do many things** / **do not do many things**.
4. They go to the playground **before** / **after** they go to the zoo.
5. When the week is over, Hanna doesn't want to **be in Spain** / **leave**.

C **Listen. Complete each sentence with a key word. Then match.**

听一听，用本单元的重点词汇补全句子，并与相应的图片配对。

1. The ______________________ is crowded.
2. Let's go to the ______________________ after school.
3. I want to go to the ______________________ today.
4. My brother is at ______________________ now.

a. ____

b. ____

c. ____

d. ____

D Listen to *Fun Trip* again. Work with a partner. Complete the table.

再听一听故事，和小伙伴一起完成表格。

	playground	zoo	post office	bank
1. Hanna	✔			
2. Rosa				
3. Rosa's mom				

E Look at D. Complete the sentences. Use *go* or *goes* in each sentence.

回顾上一题，用go或goes完成句子。

1. 

Hanna and Rosa ____go to____ ____the playground____.

2. 

Hanna and Rosa ________ ________.

3. 

Rosa's mom ________ ________.

4. 

Hanna, Rosa, and Rosa's mom ________.

MY LISTENING GOALS

☐ **I can listen to the story.** 我能听懂这个故事。

☐ **I can listen for sequence.** 我能理清事情发生的顺序。

UNIT

8 Get Ready to Listen

A Listen, point, and say. Write the words in your picture dictionary.

听一听，指一指，说一说。在“图解词典”中写出对应的单词。

amusement park

apartment

bookstore

museum

restaurant

school

B Listen and number. 听一听，在圆圈里填上正确的序号。

C Listen and complete the sentences. 听一听，并补全句子。

1. The ________________ is very large.
2. Where is the ________________?
3. I want to go to the ________________ after ________________ today.
4. After we go to the ________________, let's go to a ________________.

Listen

LISTENING GOAL: Listen for Directions 听力训练目标：明确路径

Directions tell how to go to a place. Listen for direction words and phrases like *go straight*, *walk down*, and *turn left* to know how to go to a place.
路径能告诉我们如何去一个地方。注意听go straight、walk down和turn left等用于指路的短语。

A Listen. Choose ✔ or ✘. 听一听，并判断正误。

1. 

✔ ✘

2. 

✔ ✘

3. 

✔ ✘

Come Over!

B Listen to the phone message *Come Over!*. What is it about? Choose the correct picture.
听一听这条电话留言讲了什么内容，并选择相应的图片。

A  ☐

B  ☐

Now choose ✔ or ✘. 判断正误。

1. The boy is with the friend he is speaking to. ✔ ✘
2. He is having a birthday party. ✔ ✘
3. He is giving directions to his apartment. ✔ ✘

What do the **directions** tell you?
路径告诉了你什么？

Think! Think of your last message. Who was the message from? What was it about?
想想你最近的电话留言，是谁给你留的言？留言内容是什么？

Understand

Remember!
Listen for **direction** words like *right* and *left* to know where to go.
注意听right和left等用于指路的词。

A **Think about *Come Over!*.**
Does Marco give Carla these directions? Choose Yes or No.
回想一下电话留言，马尔科有没有告诉卡拉以下路径？判断正误。

1. Walk down. **Yes** **No**
2. Turn right. **Yes** **No**

B **Listen to *Come Over!* again. Choose the correct answer.**
再听一听电话留言，选择正确的答案。

1. What is happening on Friday?
   - ☐ a. Marco's test.
   - ☐ b. Marco's birthday party.
2. What is next to Marco's apartment?
   - ☐ a. A museum.
   - ☐ b. A bookstore.
3. Where is everyone going after the amusement park?
   - ☐ a. To a museum.
   - ☐ b. To a restaurant.

C **Listen and choose the correct picture. Then write the key word.**
听一听，选择恰当的图片，并将相应的词写在下方的横线上。

1.

☐ a

☐ b

____

2.

☐ a

☐ b

____

3.

☐ a

☐ b

____

4.

☐ a

☐ b

____

D Listen to *Come Over!* again. Work with a partner. Complete the table.

再听一听电话留言，和小伙伴一起完成表格。

Place	Where	Place
1. museum	across from	restaurant
2. apartment		
3. bookstore		
4. amusement park		

E Look at D. Write directions. 回顾上一题，写出具体路径。

1.

The museum is across from a restaurant.

2.

3.

4.

MY LISTENING GOALS

- [ ] I can listen to the phone message. 我能听懂这条电话留言。
- [ ] I can listen for directions. 我能确定路径。

UNITS

7 and 8

Listening Check

Remember!
Listen for **sequence**. How can sequence help you understand a story? Listen for **directions**. What do directions tell you?
理清顺序，顺序是如何帮助你理解故事内容的？明确路径，路径告诉了你什么？

A Listen to the story *Things to Do in Town*. What is it about? Choose the correct picture.

听一听这个故事讲了什么内容，并选择相应的图片。

B Are the things in the correct order? Choose ✔ or ✘.

下列这些事的顺序对吗？判断正误。

1. To start, Dana goes to the post office. ✔ ✘
2. After the post office, she goes to the zoo. ✔ ✘
3. After the post office, she goes to a restaurant. ✔ ✘
4. At the end, she goes home. ✔ ✘

C Are these the right directions for Dana's places? Choose ✔ or ✘.

下列路径能指引达娜去她要去的地方吗？判断正误。

1. To go to the post office, turn right. ✔ ✘
2. To go to the post office, go down the street. ✔ ✘
3. To go to the restaurant, turn left. ✔ ✘
4. To go to the restaurant, turn right. ✔ ✘

D Listen to *Things to Do in Town* again. Choose the correct answer.

再听一听故事，并选择正确的答案。

1. Where does Dana want to go today?
   - ☐ a. To the amusement park.
   - ☐ b. To the museum.
   - ☐ c. To the playground.
2. Why does Dana need to go to the restaurant?
   - ☐ a. To get a letter.
   - ☐ b. To get a box.
   - ☐ c. To get some food.
3. Where is the post office?
   - ☐ a. Next to Dana's house.
   - ☐ b. Down the street.
   - ☐ c. Across the street.
4. What does Dana hear when she walks into her home?
   - ☐ a. Happy birthday!
   - ☐ b. Surprise!
   - ☐ c. Wow!
5. What is in the box?
   - ☐ a. A toy.
   - ☐ b. A balloon.
   - ☐ c. A cake.

E Listen to *Things to Do in Town* again. Complete the sentences.

再听一听故事，并补全句子。

Today is Dana's birthday. She wants to go to the (1) ____________ or the (2) ____________. But her mother gives her things to do in town. "To start, go down the street to the (3) ____________ with this letter. After that, turn right and go to the (4) ____________ next to the (5) ____________ to get food."

Dana does these things. Then she goes home. When she goes into her (6) ____________, she hears "Surprise!" It's a party! Her friends are here! Dana's mother takes the box from her. She opens it. It's a birthday cake! Dana's mother says, "I wanted you to be busy. We wanted to get ready for the party!"

UNITS 7 and 8

Get Ready to Speak

SPEAKING GOAL: Ask for and Give Directions

口语训练目标：问路和指路

When you ask for directions, you ask another person how to get to a place. When you give directions, you tell another person how to get to a place.

问路，就是询问另一个人如何到达某个地方。指路，就是告诉另一个人如何到达某个地方。

A **Read and listen to the conversation. Underline the action words that tell the man what to do.**

读一读，听一听，对话中的女士给男士指路时用了哪些单词或短语？在它们下面画横线。

Speaking Tip

Use action words like *go*, *turn*, *walk*, and *look* when you give directions.

指路时可以用go、turn、walk和look等动词。

Man: Excuse me. Can you give me directions to the post office?

Woman: Sure. Go down this street. Look for a school.

Man: OK. Then what?

Woman: Then turn right on Davis Street.

Man: Is the post office on Davis Street?

Woman: No. Go straight down Davis Street to the corner of Davis and Elm streets.

Man: OK.

Woman: Turn left onto Elm Street. The post office is on Elm Street between a bookstore and the museum.

Man: OK. Thank you very much for your help.

B **Look at A. What directions does the woman give the man? Complete the diagram.** 回顾上一题，女士是如何给男士指路的？完成思维导图。

Directions to the Post Office

1. Go down this street. → 2. ________ → 3. ________ → 4. ________

Speak

C Think about a place close to your home. Write directions. Complete the diagram.

选一个距离你家比较近的地方，怎样到那里？写出路径，完成思维导图。

Directions to ______________________

D Now write your directions. Use your ideas from **C**. Choose new words, too. Then draw a map to show the directions to get to this place.

顺着上一题的思路，写一写具体的路径，并把到那个地方的路径图画出来。

To start, ______________________

____

After that, ______________________

____

And after that, ______________________

____

Work with a partner. Ask each other about the place you chose. Then ask and give directions.

和小伙伴各选一个地方，相互问路、指路。

MY SPEAKING GOAL

☐ I can ask for and give directions.

我会问路和指路。

TOPIC

5

HEALTH

Busy, Busy, Busy!

MY GOALS

UNIT 9

- Listen to the story *Come to My House*
- Listen for setting

UNIT 10

- Listen to the article *Tips for Busy Kids*
- Listen for descriptions

SPEAK

- Give a description

A **Look at the picture. What do you see?**
看图片，回答问题。

1. Where are the children?
   What are they doing?
2. Do you think this looks like fun?
   Why or why not?

B **Listen to the Fun Fact. Then answer the questions.** 听“奇闻趣事”，回答问题。

1. Why is music good for you?
2. What do you like about music?

Think, Pair, Share
What activities do you do every week?
你每周都会参加什么活动?

UNIT

9

Get Ready to Listen

Let's learn the **key words.**
一起来学习重点词汇吧！

A Listen, point, and say. Write the words in your picture dictionary.

听一听，指一指，说一说。在“图解词典”中写出对应的短语。

go to swimming class

have a music lesson

practice violin

see a play

take an art class

write an e-mail

B Listen and draw lines. 听一听，连一连。

Mia Joe Dana Ping

C Listen and write. 听一听，写一写。

1. ______ 2. ______ 3. ______

4. ______ 5. ______ 6. ______

Listen

LISTENING GOAL: Listen for Setting 听力训练目标：明确背景

The setting is where and when something happens. Listen for time words like *eight o'clock* or *morning* and place words like *house* or *school* to know the setting.

背景就是事情发生的地点和时间。注意听表示时间的词，比如 eight o'clock、morning，以及表示地点的词，比如 house、school，它们都能提示背景。

A Listen. What do you know about the setting? Choose the correct answer.

听一听，你知道关于背景的哪些信息？圈出正确的答案。

1. I know about the **time** / **place** / **time and place**.
2. I know about the **time** / **place** / **time and place**.
3. I know about the **time** / **place** / **time and place**.

Come to My House

B Listen to the story *Come to My House*. What is it about? Choose the correct picture.

听一听这个故事讲了什么内容，并选择相应的图片。

A

B

Now put the sentences in order. 给句子排序。

a. Ray goes to Dan's house at the wrong time. ☐

b. Dan and Ray agree on a time. ☐

c. Ray tells Dan he can't come over on Friday. ☐

What is the **setting**? Does it change?
故事的背景是什么？背景有变化吗？

Think!

What activities do you do every week?
你每周都会参加什么活动？

Understand

Remember!
Listen for where and when something happens to understand the **setting**.
注意听事情发生的地点和时间，了解故事背景。

A **Think about *Come to My House*. What is the setting at the end of the story?**
回想一下故事，结尾时的背景是什么？

☐ a. Dan's house at 8:00 in the morning.
☐ b. Dan's house at 8:00 at night.

B **Listen to *Come to My House* again. Choose the correct answer.**
再听一听故事，圈出正确的答案。

1. Dan asks Ray to come to his house on **Thursday** / **Friday**.
2. On Friday after school, Ray goes to **swimming class** / **art class**.
3. On Saturday night, Dan is **having a music lesson** / **seeing a play**.
4. They are both free on **Saturday** / **Sunday**.
5. Ray thinks the agreed time is 8 o' clock **in the morning** / **in the evening**.

C **Listen. Complete each sentence with a key word. Then match.**
听一听，用本单元的重点词汇补全句子，并与相应的图片配对。

1. I ______________ every Saturday afternoon.
2. I ______________ for an hour each day.
3. Do you want to ______________ with me tonight?
4. I want to ______________ before I go to sleep.

a. ____ 

b. ____ 

c. ____ 

d. ____ 

D Listen to *Come to My House* again. Work with a partner. Complete the table. 再听一听故事，和小伙伴一起完成表格。

	Friday	Saturday morning	Saturday night	Sunday
1. When Dan is not busy	✓			
2. When Ray is not busy				
3. When Dan and Ray are not busy				

E Look at **D**. Answer each question with *Yes, I can* or *I'm sorry. I can't*.
回顾上一题，用Yes, I can或I'm sorry. I can't回答问题。

1.

Dan: Can you come to my house on Friday?

Ray: I'm sorry. I can't.

2.

Ray: Can you play on Saturday morning?

Dan: ____________________

3.

Ray: Can you play on Saturday night?

Dan: ____________________

4.

Dan: Can you come to my house on Sunday?

Ray: ____________________

MY LISTENING GOALS

☐ I can listen to the story.
我能听懂这个故事。

☐ I can listen for the setting.
我能搞清楚故事的背景。

UNIT
10 Get Ready to Listen

A Listen, point, and say. Write the words in your picture dictionary.
听一听，指一指，说一说。在“图解词典”中写出对应的短语。

go for a walk

have fun

listen to music

make a model

play a board game

take a nap

B Listen and number. 听一听，在圆圈里填上正确的序号。

C Listen and complete the sentences. 听一听，并补全句子。

1. Ben and his parents ________________ every night.
2. I want to ________________ of my favorite car.
3. My older sister and her friends like to ________________ and ________________.
4. After they ________________, they want to ________________.

Listen

LISTENING GOAL: Listen for Descriptions 听力训练目标：听清描述性词语

A description tells how something looks, feels, sounds, and tastes. Listen for description words like *busy, fun, quiet,* and *good.* 描述性词语能告诉我们某物看起来、摸起来、听起来、尝起来是什么样的。注意听像busy、fun、quiet和good这样的词，它们都是描述性词语。

A Listen. Choose ✔ or ✘. 听一听，并判断正误。

1. 
✔ ✘

2. 
✔ ✘

3. 
✔ ✘

Tips for Busy Kids

B Listen to the article *Tips for Busy Kids*. What is it about? Choose the correct picture.
听一听这篇文章讲了什么内容，并选择相应的图片。

A 

B 

Now choose ✔ or ✘. 判断正误。

1. The article is about how to stay busy. ✔ ✘
2. Always being busy makes you feel good. ✔ ✘
3. There are different ways to have quiet time. ✔ ✘

Think!
How do you have quiet time?
你都是如何度过属于自己的安静时间的？

What **descriptions** are in the article?
文章中有哪些描述性词语？

Understand

Remember!
To know what something is like, listen for **description words** such as *busy*, *fun*, *quiet*, and *good*.
想知道某样东西是什么样的，就要注意听描述性词语，比如busy、fun、quiet和good。

A **Think about *Tips for Busy Kids*.**
Are there description words for these things?
Choose Yes or No.
回想一下文章，里面有没有描述下列事物的词语？判断正误。

1. School, friends, and model. **Yes** **No**
2. Flowers, birds, and music. **Yes** **No**

B **Listen to *Tips for Busy Kids* again. Choose the correct answer.**
再听一听文章，选择正确的答案。

1. What can happen when you get very tired?
   - ☐ a. You can get bored.
   - ☐ b. You can get sick.
2. What does the article say you should have every day?
   - ☐ a. Quiet time.
   - ☐ b. A nap.
3. What kind of music does the article talk about?
   - ☐ a. Loud.
   - ☐ b. Beautiful.

C **Listen and choose the correct picture. Then write the key word.**
听一听，选择恰当的图片，并将相应的词写在下方的横线上。

1.

☐ a

☐ b
____

2.

☐ a

☐ b
____

3.

☐ a

☐ b
____

4.

☐ a

☐ b
____

D Listen to *Tips for Busy Kids* again. Work with a partner. Complete the table.

再听一听文章，和小伙伴一起完成表格。

Action Word	Description Word	Thing
1. go	nice	walk
2.		board game
3.		music
4.		nap

E Look at D. Write sentences using description words.

回顾上一题，用描述性词语描述图片。

1. 

Go for a nice walk.

2. 

3. 

4. 

MY LISTENING GOALS

- ☐ **I can listen to the article.** 我能听懂这篇文章。
- ☐ **I can listen for descriptions.** 我能听清描述性词语。

UNITS 9 and 10

Listening Check

Remember!
Listen for **setting**. What does the setting tell you? Listen for **description words**. What do description words tell you?
明确背景，背景告诉了你哪些信息？听清描述性词语，这些词语告诉了你什么？

A Listen to the radio advertisement *A Place for Fun*. What is it about? Choose the correct picture.

听一听这则电台广告讲了什么内容，并选择相应的图片。

A

B

C

B Which are true statements about the setting? Choose ✔ or ✘.

下列句子中对背景的介绍正确吗？根据你听到的内容判断正误。

1. The time is the morning. ✔ ✘
2. The time is the afternoon. ✔ ✘
3. The place is an art class. ✔ ✘
4. The place is a swim class. ✔ ✘

C Which words are used to describe each place? Choose ✔ or ✘.

下列句子中对不同地方的描述正确吗？根据你听到的内容判断正误。

1. The theater is beautiful. ✔ ✘
2. The pool is small. ✔ ✘
3. The art class is great. ✔ ✘
4. The projects are boring. ✔ ✘

D Listen to *A Place for Fun* again. Choose the correct answer.

再听一听电台广告，并选择正确的答案。

1. What is the radio advertisement about?
   - ☐ a. A school.
   - ☐ b. A town center building.
   - ☐ c. A theater.
2. What is something you can do there?
   - ☐ a. See a play.
   - ☐ b. See a movie.
   - ☐ c. Play soccer.
3. How many students are in the art class?
   - ☐ a. Eight.
   - ☐ b. Nine.
   - ☐ c. Ten.
4. What does Ryan say about the art projects?
   - ☐ a. They are interesting.
   - ☐ b. They are difficult.
   - ☐ c. They are long.
5. What does Ryan say the students do every week?
   - ☐ a. Make a model.
   - ☐ b. Have fun.
   - ☐ c. See a play.

E Listen to *A Place for Fun* again. Complete the sentences.

再听一听电台广告，并补全句子。

Man: Welcome to our town center building! It's Monday afternoon, and there is so much to do here. You can (1) ________ in our beautiful theater or (2) ________ in our quiet computer room. You can (3) ________ in the music room or (4) ________ in our big, new pool! Let's visit our after-school art class. Ten students are (5) ________ here this afternoon. Let's talk to Ryan. Ryan, can you tell us what you think about this art class?

Ryan: It's great! We do really interesting projects. And every week we (6) ________.

Man: Thanks, Ryan! Come down to the town center building and have some fun with us!

UNITS **9** and **10**

Get Ready to Speak

SPEAKING GOAL: Give a Description 口语训练目标：描述事物

A description tells how something looks, feels, sounds, or tastes. To give a description, use words that give more information.

描述事物就是叙述某样东西看起来、摸起来、听起来或者尝起来是什么样的。描述的时候，要选择能传达更多信息的词。

A **Read and listen to the description. Underline the description words.**

读一读，听一听，在描述性词语下面画横线。

Speaking Tip

Use description words like *hard*, *interesting*, and *small* before a person, place, or thing.

描述某人、某地或某物的时候，可以在前面加上描述性词语，比如hard、interesting、small。

Hi. I'm Greg. I love making interesting models. It takes a lot of time and hard work. But it is fun work.

I started making them when I was five. Those models were small and easy because they only had a few pieces.

I make much more difficult models now. They have many small pieces!

B **Look at A. What description words does Greg use to describe each of these things? Complete the diagram.**

回顾上一题，格雷格在描述下列事物的时候，用了哪些描述性词语？完成思维导图。

Description words

- the activity — 1. hard
- doing it as a young child — 2. ______
- doing it now — 3. ______

Speak

C Think about your favorite activity. Write description words to describe it. Complete the diagram.

想一想，你最喜欢参加什么活动？用描述性词语写一写这项活动，完成思维导图。

Description words

- your favorite activity: ____________
- when you started the activity: ____________
- now: ____________

D Now write a description of your favorite activity. Use your ideas from **C**. Choose new words, too. Then draw the activity.

顺着上一题的思路，描述一下你最喜欢参加的活动，并把这项活动画出来。

I love ____________

It is ____________ and ____________

When I started doing this activity, it was

____

Now it is ____________

Work with a partner. Ask your partner about his or her favorite activity. Then tell your partner about your favorite activity.

问一问你的小伙伴最喜欢什么活动，各自描述一下自己喜欢参加的活动。

MY SPEAKING GOAL

☐ I can give a description.

我会描述事物。

TOPIC
6
HISTORY

Home Sweet Home

MY GOALS

UNIT 11

- Listen to the story *The Mirror*
- Listen for what is similar

UNIT 12

- Listen to the article *Then and Now*
- Listen for what is different

SPEAK

- Make a comparison

A **Look at the picture. What do you see?**
看图片，回答问题。

1. Where is this?
2. Do you want to live there? Why or why not?

FUN FACT

Listen

A Time Before Houses

B **Listen to the Fun Fact. Then answer the questions.**
听“奇闻趣事”，回答问题。

1. How did people live thousands of years before now?
2. Do you think this was a good way to live? Why or why not?

Think, Pair, Share
What is your home like?
你的家是什么样子的？

UNIT 11

Get Ready to Listen

Let's learn the **key words**.
一起来学习重点词汇吧！

A **Listen, point, and say. Write the words in your picture dictionary.**
听一听，指一指，说一说。在“图解词典”中写出对应的单词。

brush

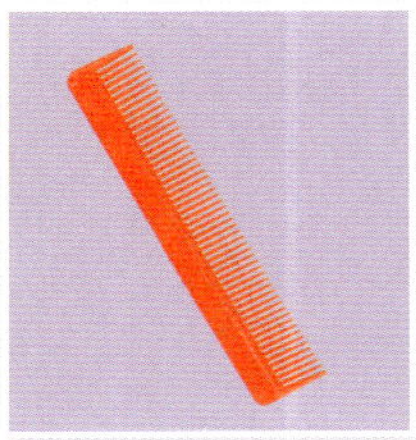
comb

garden

mirror

sink

stairs

B **Listen and draw lines.** 听一听，连一连。

Sara **Joy** **Mark** **Leo**

C **Listen and write.** 听一听，写一写。

1. ______ 2. ______ 3. ______
4. ______ 5. ______ 6. ______

Listen

LISTENING GOAL: Listen for What Is Similar 听力训练目标：听清相似之处

When two things are almost the same, they are similar.
Listen for words like *both, too,* and *also* to find what is similar.
两种事物几乎相同就是相似。注意听both、too和also等用于表示相似的词。

A **Listen. Then complete the sentences.** 听一听，并补全句子。

1. Sofia and Daniel both live in ______ houses.
2. Aisha and Jess both have ______ people in their family.
3. We both grow ______ in our garden.

The Mirror

B **Listen to the story *The Mirror*. What is it about? Choose the correct picture.**
听一听这个故事讲了什么内容，并选择相应的图片。

A

B

Now put the sentences in order. 给句子排序。

a. Peter moves to a new house. ☐

b. Peter sees that he is the boy in the mirror. ☐

c. Peter sees another boy and runs away. ☐

What things are similar in the story?
故事中的哪些东西是相似的?

Think!

What do you think is funny about the story?
你觉得这个故事的哪个部分比较有趣?

Understand

Remember!
Listen for words like *both*, *too*, and *also* to find what is **similar**.
注意听both、too和also等用于表示相似的词。

A **Think about *The Mirror*.**
How are Peter and the other boy similar?
回想一下故事，皮特和另一个男孩在哪些地方相似?

- [ ] a. They both have blue eyes, a big nose, and brown hair.
- [ ] b. They both have blue eyes, small ears, and blond hair.

B **Listen to *The Mirror* again. Choose the correct answer.**
再听一听故事，圈出正确的答案。

1. Peter sees **a man** / **another boy** in the mirror.
2. The boy has **big** / **small** ears.
3. The boy has **blond** / **brown** hair.
4. Peter **talks to** / **runs away from** the boy.
5. Peter sees that he is looking in the **sink** / **mirror**.

C **Listen. Complete each sentence with a key word. Then match.**
听一听，用本单元的重点词汇补全句子，并与相应的图片配对。

1. I like your ____________.
2. Where is the ____________?
3. I have a black ____________, too.
4. That is a small ____________.

a. ____ 

b. ____ 

c. ____ 

d. ____ 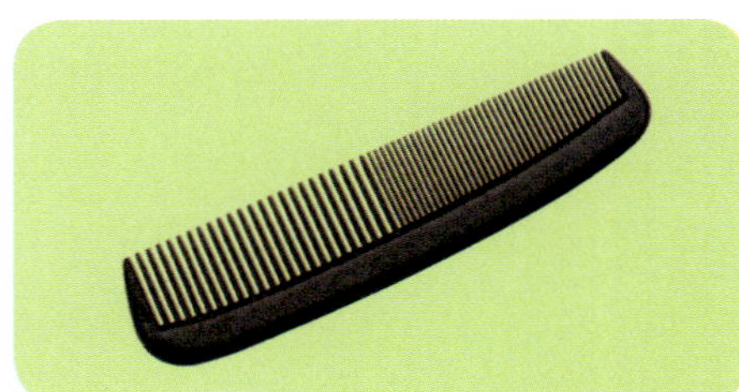

D Listen to *The Mirror* again. Work with a partner. Complete the diagram.

再听一听故事，和小伙伴一起完成思维导图。

They both have ...

1. blue eyes
2. ______
3. ______
4. ______

E Look at D. Complete the sentences. Use *Peter and the boy both have*.

参照上一题，用Peter and the boy both have完成句子。

1. 

Peter and the boy both have blue eyes.

2. 

______

3. 

______

4. 

______

MY LISTENING GOALS

- [ ] I can listen to the story. 我能听懂这个故事。
- [ ] I can listen for what is similar. 我能听清事物的相似之处。

UNIT

12

Get Ready to Listen

Let's learn the **key words**.

一起来学习重点词汇吧！

A Listen, point, and say. Write the words in your picture dictionary.

听一听，指一指，说一说。在“图解词典”中写出对应的单词。

armchair

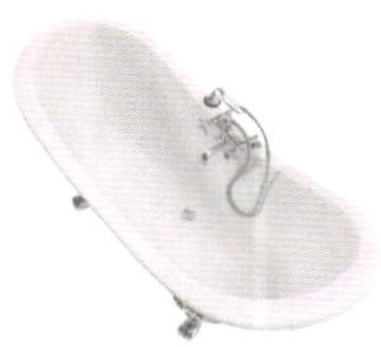

bathtub

oven

refrigerator

rug

sofa

B Listen and number. 听一听，在圆圈里填上正确的序号。

C Listen and complete the sentences. 听一听，并补全句子。

1. Ed doesn't have a ____________ in his house.
2. That ____________ is very nice.
3. We use our ____________ and ____________ every day.
4. We have the same ____________ and ____________!

Listen

LISTENING GOAL: Listen for What Is Different 听力训练目标：听清不同之处

When two things are not the same, they are different. Listen for words like *but, not,* and *unlike* to find what is different.

两种不一样的事物就是不同的。注意听 but、not 和 unlike 等用于表示不同的词。

A Listen. Choose ✔ or ✘. 听一听，并判断正误。

1.  ✔ ✘

2.  ✔ ✘

3.  ✔ ✘

Then and Now

B Listen to the article *Then and Now*. What is it about? Choose the correct picture.

听一听这篇文章讲了什么内容，并选择相应的图片。

A  ☐

B  ☐

Now choose ✔ or ✘. 判断正误。

1. The article talks about homes now and homes in 1500. ✔ ✘
2. The article says many things are the same now and in 1500. ✔ ✘
3. People cooked food in different ways in 1500. ✔ ✘

Think! Do you want to live in 1500? Why or why not?
你愿意生活在1500年吗？为什么？

How are the things in our homes **different** from 1500?
和1500年相比，人们家里的东西有什么不同？

Understand

Remember!
Listen for words like *but*, *not*, and *unlike* to find what is **different**.
注意听but、not和unlike等用于表示不同的词。

A **Think about *Then and Now*. Did people do these things in 1500? Choose Yes or No.**
回想一下文章，生活在1500年的人们会做下面的事情吗？判断正误。

1. People kept food cold with no refrigerators. **Yes** **No**
2. People cooked food in ovens. **Yes** **No**

B **Listen to *Then and Now* again. Choose the correct answer.**
再听一听文章，选择正确的答案。

1. What does the article say looks nice in our homes?
   - ☐ a. Sofas.
   - ☐ b. Rugs.
2. In 1500, what did people sit on?
   - ☐ a. Wood chairs.
   - ☐ b. Sofas.
3. What did people wash with in 1500?
   - ☐ a. Rain and a leaf.
   - ☐ b. Water and an old piece of clothing.

C **Listen and choose the correct picture. Then write the key word.**
听一听，选择恰当的图片，并将相应的词写在下方的横线上。

1.

☐ a

☐ b

____

2.

☐ a

☐ b

____

3.

☐ a

☐ b

____

4.

☐ a

☐ b

____

D Listen to *Then and Now* again. Work with a partner. Complete the table.

再听一听文章，和小伙伴一起完成表格。

Today	In 1500
ovens	1. fire
refrigerators	2.
sofas	3.
bathtubs	4.

E Look at D. Write. Use *but*. 回顾上一题，用but完成句子。

1.

Today people use ovens,

but in 1500 they used fire.

2.

Today people use refrigerators,

______________________.

3.

Today people use sofas,

______________________.

4.

Today people use bathtubs,

______________________.

MY LISTENING GOALS

- [ ] I can listen to the article. 我能听懂这篇文章。
- [ ] I can listen for what is different. 我能听清事物的不同之处。

UNITS **11** and **12**

Listening Check

Remember!
Listen for words like *both*, *too*, and *also* to know what is **similar**. Listen for words like *but*, *not*, and *unlike* to know what is **different**.
注意听both、too和also，找到事物的相似之处。注意听but、not和unlike，找到事物的不同之处。

A Listen to the passage *Just Like Us*. What is it about? Choose the correct picture.

听一听这篇文章讲了什么内容，并选择相应的图片。

A
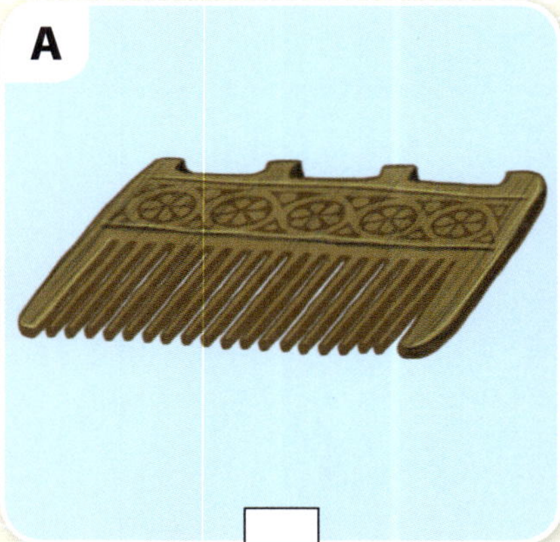
☐

B

☐

C
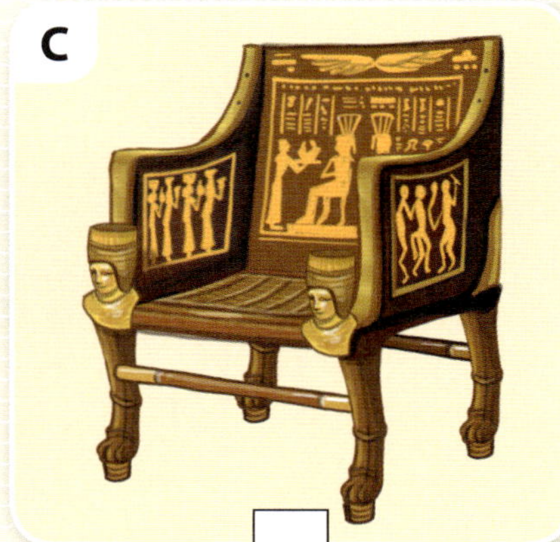
☐

B How were people in Egypt 5,000 years before now similar to us? Choose ✔ or ✘.

5000年前的埃及人的生活和我们的有哪些相似之处？判断正误。

1. They had refrigerators. ✔ ✘
2. They wanted to look good. ✔ ✘
3. They had bathtubs. ✔ ✘
4. They had gardens. ✔ ✘

C How were people in Egypt different from us? Choose ✔ or ✘.

5000年前的埃及人的生活和我们的有哪些不同之处？判断正误。

1. They cooked with different ovens. ✔ ✘
2. They used combs. ✔ ✘
3. They washed in rivers. ✔ ✘
4. They used mirrors. ✔ ✘

D Listen to *Just Like Us* again. Choose the correct answer.

再听一听文章，并选择正确的答案。

1. People in Egypt 5,000 years before now were _____.

   ☐ a. very different from us ☐ b. a little different from us ☐ c. not different from us

2. What does the passage say people in Egypt 5,000 years before now cared about?

   ☐ a. How they looked. ☐ b. How they cooked. ☐ c. How they walked.

3. For combs, people in Egypt 5,000 years before now used _____.

   ☐ a. parts of trees ☐ b. food ☐ c. their hands

4. What is the same about us and people in Egypt 5,000 years before now?

   ☐ a. Using ovens. ☐ b. Using bathtubs. ☐ c. Using combs.

5. To wash their bodies, people in Egypt 5,000 years before now used _____.

   ☐ a. rivers ☐ b. bathtubs ☐ c. sinks

E Listen to *Just Like Us* again. Complete the sentences.

再听一听文章，并补全句子。

People in Egypt 5,000 years before now were different from us in many ways. Their (1) ____________ were very different. They didn't have (2) ____________. But they were similar to us too. We want to look good. This was true for them too! We use (3) ____________. They used them too. They used parts of trees for their combs. There were no (4) ____________, but they washed themselves in the river. They also used (5) ____________. We have (6) ____________, and they did too. In many ways, they were just like us!

UNITS 11 and 12

Get Ready to Speak

SPEAKING GOAL: Make a Comparison 口语训练目标：做比较

When you make a comparison, you say how one thing is like or not like another.

做比较的时候，要说出事物的相同点和不同点。

A Read and listen to the passage. Underline the phrases for making comparisons.

读一读，听一听，在用于表示比较的单词和短语下面画横线。

Speaking Tip

To make a comparison, use phrases like *as well*, *similarly*, and *on the other hand*.

可以用as well、similarly和on the other hand来表示比较。

Welcome Home by Hoshi Ito

My home is new. My family just moved to it last year. In some ways, it is like our old home. There was a garden at the back of our old home. Similarly, there is a garden at the back of my new home. On the other hand, some things are different in the new home. In the old home, there was a very big living room with big windows. The living room in our new home is small. On the other hand, I have my own room for the first time in the new home. I'm very excited about that!

B Look at **A**. How does Ito compare her new home to her old home? Complete the diagram.

回顾上一题，井门是如何比较自己的新家和旧家的？完成思维导图。

Ito's New Home	Both	Ito's Old Home
1. small living room	3. ______	4. ______
2. ______		5. ______

Speak

C Think about your home. Compare it to an old home or a friend's home. Complete the diagram. 想一想你现在的家，把它和你以前的家，或者朋友的家做比较，并完成思维导图。

My Home	Both	Other Home
______	______	______
______	______	______
______	______	______

D Now write about your home. Use your ideas from **C**. Choose new words, too. Then draw your home.
顺着上一题的思路，比较一下两个家，并把你的家画出来。

My home is ______________________

____

Similarly, ______________________

____

On the other hand, ______________________

____

Ask your partner about his or her home. Then tell about your home and compare it to another home you know.
和小伙伴相互介绍一下各自的家，然后比较一下你们的家。

MY SPEAKING GOAL

☐ I can make a comparison.
我会做比较。

Listening WITH Speaking 3

Workbook

WORKBOOK

UNIT

1

Listen

LISTENING GOAL:

Listen and Take Notes

听力训练目标：听录音，做笔记

Remember!

Notes are words or phrases you write down as you listen. **Notes** help you remember important information.

笔记是你听录音时所做的记录。笔记可以帮助你记下重要信息。

A Listen to the story *The Zookeeper's Problem*. What is it about? Take notes.

听一听这个故事讲了什么内容，在下面做笔记。

Notes

____

____

____

____

B Think about *The Zookeeper's Problem*. What is a good note? Choose ✔ or ✘.

回想一下故事，下列哪些笔记记得好？判断一下。

1. The panda won't come out. (✔) ✘
2. One of the visitors is a news reporter. ✔ ✘
3. The musician is a woman. ✔ ✘

C Listen to *The Zookeeper's Problem* again. Choose the correct answer.

再听一听故事，选择正确的答案。

1. Where is the panda?
   - [x] a. In a van.
   - [ ] b. In a car.
   - [ ] c. In a box.
2. What does the zookeeper bring the animal?
   - [ ] a. A toy.
   - [ ] b. A friend.
   - [ ] c. Food.
3. Who helps?
   - [ ] a. The news reporter.
   - [ ] b. A visitor.
   - [ ] c. Another animal.
4. What does the musician play?
   - [ ] a. A fun game.
   - [ ] b. Beautiful music.
   - [ ] c. Loud music.

D Listen and write the word. Then choose the correct picture.

听一听，写出正确的单词或短语，并选择相应的图片。

1. ______tailor______

 ☑ a

 ☐ b

2. ____________

 ☐ a

 ☐ b

3. ____________

 ☐ a

 ☐ b

4. ____________

 ☐ a

 ☐ b

E Complete the sentences. 选一选，填一填。

news reporter	~~driver~~	musician	judge	tailor	scientist

1. The ______driver______ knows all of the roads in the neighborhood.
2. The ____________ plays the drums and the piano.
3. The ____________ studies animals.
4. The ____________ can fix your pants.

F Unscramble and write. 理一理，写出正确的单词。

1. g e d j u

______judge______

2. e i r v d r

____

3. c s t i e n t i s

____

4. o r i l t a

____

WORKBOOK
UNIT
2

Listen

LISTENING GOAL:
Listen for the 5 Ws
听力训练目标：听清5个W（五要素）

Remember!
Asking yourself the **5Ws** after you listen will help you know the most important information.
听录音中的5个W分别是什么，掌握听力材料中的重要信息。

A Listen to the passage ***Mechanic to Astronaut***.
Then put the pictures in order. 听一听这篇文章，给图片排序。

A
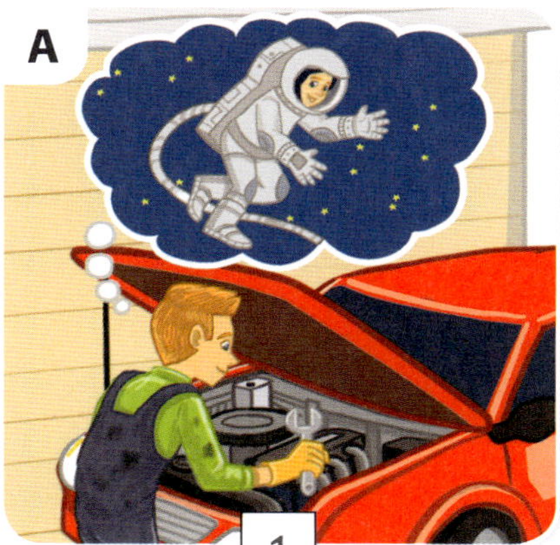
1

B
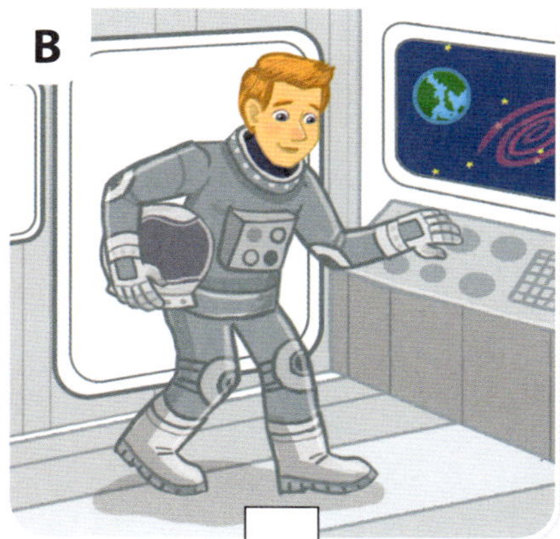
☐

C

☐

B Think about ***Mechanic to Astronaut***. Which W questions are answered in the passage? Choose ✔ or ✘.
回想一下文章，录音中回答了下列哪些问题？判断一下。

1. What do mechanics do? (✔) ✘
2. Where did he take the test? ✔ ✘
3. When is he in space? ✔ ✘

C Listen to ***Mechanic to Astronaut*** again. Choose Yes or No.
再听一听文章，判断正误。

1. Andrew Jay Feustel fixed buses. **Yes** **(No)**
2. He wanted to be an astronaut. **Yes** **No**
3. Now he is a news reporter. **Yes** **No**
4. He lives in space. **Yes** **No**
5. He works with scientists. **Yes** **No**
6. He fixes things in space. **Yes** **No**

D Listen. Then read and choose the correct answer.

听一听，读一读，并选择正确的答案。

1. Who writes many books?

a. 

(b.) 

c. 

2. Who has a dollar?

a. 

b. 

c. 

3. Who works in a factory?

a. 

b. 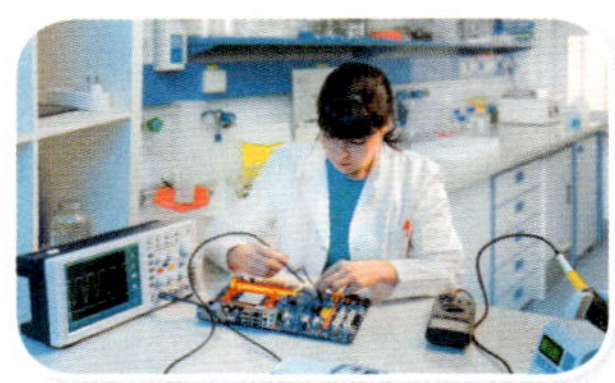

c. 

E Complete the missing words. 根据首字母提示，用本单元的重点词汇补全句子。

1. Many people are listening to the singer__________.
2. The a__________ is in space.
3. The m__________ is fixing the car.
4. The e__________ is helping to build a bridge.

Remember!
Ask for more information using the **5 Ws**:
who, *what*, *when*, *where*, and *why*.
用5个W询问更多信息，即who (什么人)、what (是什么)、when (什么时间)、where (在哪里) 和 why (为什么)。

Speak

Circle the W words in the questions.
Then think of your own questions with W words. Tell your partner.

把问句中以 W 开头的疑问词圈出来，然后试着用这些疑问词造句，跟小伙伴说一说。

Who is she? What is her job?

Where does she work?

WORKBOOK

UNIT 3

Listen

LISTENING GOAL: Listen for Facts

听力训练目标：明确事实

Remember!
A **fact** is something that is true for everyone. Listen for **facts** to know what is true in a listening.
事实就是真实情况，对每个人来说都是如此。听录音，明确哪些是事实。

A Listen to the passage ***Before Calculators***. What do you hear about? Choose ✔ or ✘.

听一听这篇文章讲了什么内容，判断正误。

1. 

The stapler. ☐ ✔ ☐ ✘

2. 

The abacus. ☐ ✔ ☐ ✘

B Think about ***Before Calculators***. What facts do you hear? Choose ✔ or ✘.

回想一下文章，下列哪些句子说的是事实？判断正误。

1. We use a dictionary to learn new words. ☐ ✔ ☐ ✘
2. There were calculators before abacuses. ☐ ✔ ☐ ✘
3. An abacus has sticks. ☐ ✔ ☐ ✘

C Listen to ***Before Calculators*** again. Choose the correct answer.

再听一听文章，选择正确的答案。

1. What do we use to do math today?
   - ☐ a. An abacus.
   - ☐ b. A calculator.
   - ☐ c. A dictionary.
2. Where was the abacus used?
   - ☐ a. In Thailand.
   - ☐ b. In Italy.
   - ☐ c. In Egypt.
3. What is an abacus made of?
   - ☐ a. Sticks and beads.
   - ☐ b. Stones and beads.
   - ☐ c. Beads only.
4. How many beads are on each stick?
   - ☐ a. Five.
   - ☐ b. Seven.
   - ☐ c. One.

D Listen and write the word. Then choose the correct picture.

听一听，写出正确的单词，并选择相应的图片。

1. ______________________

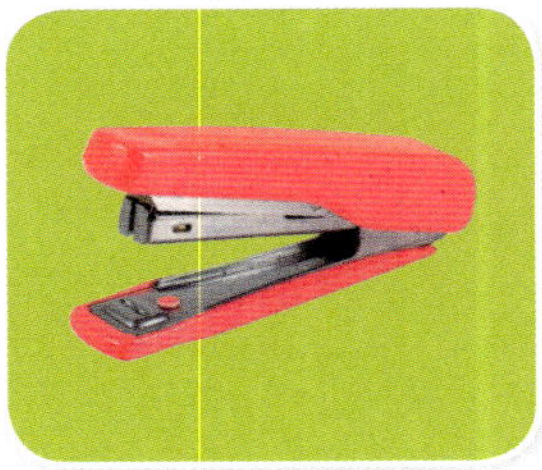

☐ a

☐ b

2. ______________________

☐ a

☐ b

3. ______________________

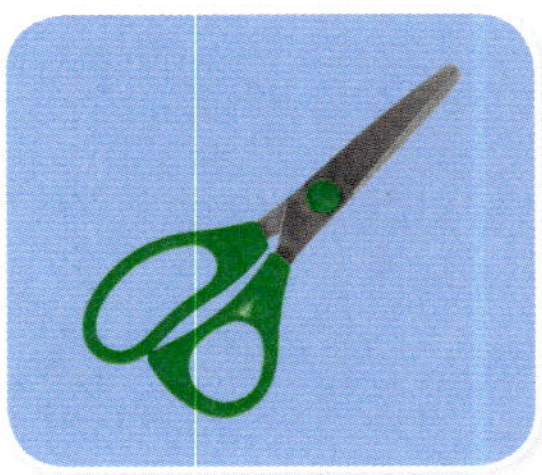

☐ a

☐ b

4. ______________________

☐ a

☐ b

E Complete the sentences. 选一选，填一填。

workbook	folder	dictionary	calculator	stapler	scissors

1. The students write their homework in their ______________________.
2. I use a ______________________ to help me with math.
3. You can use ______________________ to cut the paper.
4. I put all my work in my ______________________.

F Unscramble and write. 理一理，写出正确的单词。

1. i o c t d i r y n a

____

2. a t p r l s e

____

3. o f r e l d

____

4. k o b o r w o k

____

WORKBOOK UNIT 4

Listen

LISTENING GOAL: Listen for Opinions

听力训练目标：明确观点

Remember!
An **opinion** is what a person thinks about something. It is not true for everyone. Listen for **opinions** to know how people feel.
观点就是一个人对事物或问题的看法，每个人的观点不尽相同。听录音，明确观点，了解人们的看法。

A Listen to the story *The Visit*. Then put the pictures in order.

听一听这个故事，给图片排序。

A

☐

B

☐

C

☐

B Think about *The Visit*. Which is an opinion? Choose ✔ or ✘.

回想一下故事，下列哪个句子表达的是观点？判断正误。

1. They open a laptop. ✔ ✘
2. China was very interesting. ✔ ✘
3. They fall asleep again. ✔ ✘

C Listen to *The Visit* again. Choose Yes or No.

再听一听故事，判断正误。

1. Jen and Al are studying China. **Yes** **No**
2. They are using a tablet. **Yes** **No**
3. They wake up in China. **Yes** **No**
4. The students ask questions about Brazil. **Yes** **No**
5. Al and Jen think China was boring. **Yes** **No**
6. They put the laptop away. **Yes** **No**

D Listen. Then read and choose the correct answer.

听一听，读一读，并选择正确的答案。

1. What does each child in class have?

a.  b.  c. 

2. What is on the wall of the classroom?

a.  b.  c. 

3. Where are the books?

a.  b.  c. 

E Complete the missing words. 根据首字母提示，用本单元的重点词汇补全句子。

1. My country's f____________ is red and white.
2. He uses the Internet on his l____________.
3. What is in the d____________?
4. The workbooks are in the c____________.

Remember!
Use phrases like *you're right* to **agree** and *I don't think so* to **disagree**.
用you're right表示赞同，用I don't think so表示反对。

Speak

Circle the phrase that shows a person agrees.
Underline the phrase that shows a person disagrees.
Then tell a partner your opinion.

把表示赞同的句子圈出来，在表示反对的句子下面画横线，然后跟小伙伴说一说你的观点。

Beth: I like using laptops in class. I think they help us learn.

John: You're right. They are helpful!

Sara: I don't think so. I think tablets are more helpful.

WORKBOOK

UNIT

5

Listen

LISTENING GOAL:

Listen for Preferences

听力训练目标：明确偏好

Remember!
Listen for *I prefer* and *I like* to know about **preferences**.
注意听I prefer和I like，它们常用于表达偏好。

A **Listen to the article *Clothing Then and Now*. What do you hear about? Choose ✔ or ✘.**

听一听这篇文章，你听到了什么内容？判断正误。

1. 

Clothes in 1980. ✔ ✘

2. 

Clothes in 1890. ✔ ✘

B **Think about *Clothing Then and Now*. What clothes did people prefer in 1890? Choose ✔ or ✘.**

回想一下文章，1890年的人们更喜欢什么样的衣服？判断正误。

1. They liked long coats. ✔ ✘
2. They liked blue coats. ✔ ✘
3. They liked sneakers. ✔ ✘

C **Listen to *Clothing Then and Now* again. Choose the correct answer.**

再听一听文章，选择正确的答案。

1. In 1890, people liked ________________ hats.
   ☐ a. small ☐ b. warm ☐ c. big
2. Today, people wear ________________.
   ☐ a. heavy hats ☐ b. small hats ☐ c. big hats
3. There were no ________________ in 1890.
   ☐ a. handbags ☐ b. sneakers ☐ c. bathing suits
4. In 1890, most coats were ________________.
   ☐ a. black ☐ b. blue ☐ c. short

D Listen and write the word. Then choose the correct picture.

听一听，写出正确的单词，并选择相应的图片。

1. ______________________

☐ a

☐ b

2. ______________________

☐ a

☐ b

3. ______________________

☐ a

☐ b

4. ______________________

☐ a

☐ b

E Complete the sentences. 选一选，填一填。

handbag	coat	baseball cap	sneakers	swimsuit	shorts

1. I can run fast with these ______________.
2. I can't go in the water because I don't have a ______________.
3. My mother has her keys and her money in her ______________.
4. It is too hot to wear a ______________.

F Unscramble and write. 理一理，写出正确的单词。

1. u w i m s i t s

____

2. o t s h r s

____

3. e a l b l a s b a p c

____

4. a d g b a n h

____

WORKBOOK

UNIT

6

Listen

LISTENING GOAL:

Listen for Reasons

听力训练目标：明确原因

Remember!

Listen for *because* to find the **reason** why people do or feel something.

注意听because引导的句子，了解人们做某事或者产生某种感受的原因。

A Listen to the story *The New Coat*. Then put the pictures in order.

听一听这个故事，给图片排序。

A

☐

B

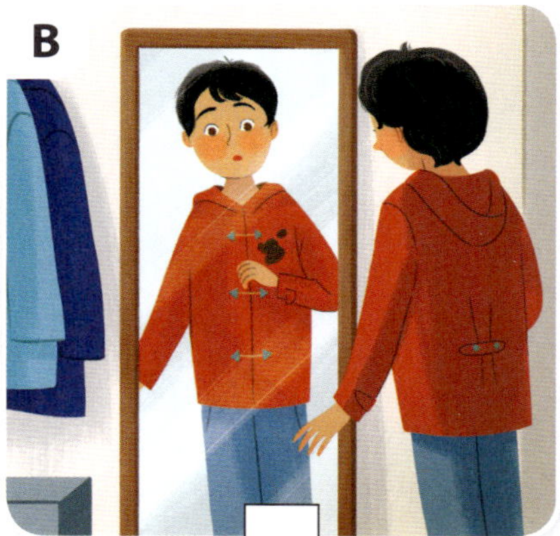

☐

C

☐

B Think about *The New Coat*. What are some of the reasons you hear? Choose ✔ or ✘. 回想一下故事，下列句子中陈述的原因正确吗？判断正误。

1. Amal thinks the coat is heavy because he's wearing two coats. ✔ ✘
2. Amal thinks the coat is dirty because the mirror is dirty. ✔ ✘
3. Amal's father laughs because the coat is big. ✔ ✘

C Listen to *The New Coat* again. Choose Yes or No.

再听一听故事，判断正误。

1. Amal goes shopping for new sneakers. **Yes** **No**
2. Amal goes shopping with his father. **Yes** **No**
3. Amal's father asks him to try on a coat. **Yes** **No**
4. Amal tries on the coat over his own coat. **Yes** **No**
5. The coat is dirty. **Yes** **No**
6. The mirror is dirty. **Yes** **No**

D Listen. Then read and choose the correct answer.

听一听，读一读，并选择正确的答案。

1. What is Jan's new book like?

a.  b.  c. 

2. How are Taro's sneakers?

a.  b.  c. 

3. What are my pants like?

a.  b.  c. 

E Write the missing letters. 根据首字母提示，用本单元的重点词汇补全句子。

1. I'm cold because my coat is too t____________.
2. My mother just washed these shorts, so they're c____________.
3. You can't wear d____________ clothes to school.
4. This workbook has a lot of pages. It's very t____________.

Speak

Remember!
Use the words *I prefer* and *I like* with *because* to give **preferences**.
用I prefer和I like表达偏好，用because说明理由。

Circle the words *prefer*, *like*, and *because* in the sentences. Then think of your own sentence to give preferences. Tell your partner.

把下列句子中的 prefer、like 和 because 圈出来，然后用这些词造句，表达你的偏好，并跟小伙伴说一说。

I like the blue shorts because they are my favorite color.

My mother prefers to shop online because it is fast.

Listen

LISTENING GOAL:
Listen for Sequence
听力训练目标：理清顺序

Remember!
The **sequence** is the order things happen. Listen for **sequence** words to understand order.
顺序就是事情发生的先后次序。注意听表示顺序的词，了解事情发生的先后顺序。

A Listen to the story ***Where Is It?***. What do you hear about?
Choose ✔ or ✘. 听一听这个故事，你听到了什么内容？判断正误。

1. 

Rabbit and her books. ☐ ✔ ☐ ✘

2. 

Rabbit and her gold. ☐ ✔ ☐ ✘

B Think about ***Where Is It?***. What is the sequence of the story?
Choose ✔ or ✘. 回想一下故事，事情发生的顺序是什么？判断正误。

1. To start, Wolf looks for the gold at the zoo. ☐ ✔ ☐ ✘
2. To start, Wolf looks for the gold in Rabbit's home. ☐ ✔ ☐ ✘
3. After that, Wolf looks for the gold at the zoo. ☐ ✔ ☐ ✘

C Listen to ***Where Is It?*** again. Choose the correct answer.
再听一听故事，选择正确的答案。

1. At the start of the story, where does Rabbit say her gold is?
   ☐ a. In the bank. ☐ b. In a safe place. ☐ c. At the zoo.
2. After looking for the gold in Rabbit's home, where does Wolf look next?
   ☐ a. At the zoo. ☐ b. At the playground. ☐ c. In the bank.
3. Who does Wolf see at the zoo?
   ☐ a. Lion. ☐ b. Bear. ☐ c. Zebra.
4. Where does Rabbit keep her gold?
   ☐ a. At her home. ☐ b. At the zoo. ☐ c. At the bank.

D Listen and write the word. Then choose the correct picture.

听一听，写出正确的单词，并选择相应的图片。

1. ______________________

☐ a

☐ b

2. ______________________

☐ a

☐ b

3. ______________________

☐ a

☐ b

4. ______________________

☐ a

☐ b

E Complete the sentences. 选一选，填一填。

airport	zoo	home	post office	bank	playground

1. People put money in the ______________.
2. You can fly to many places from the ______________.
3. I like to watch TV and be with my family at ______________.
4. There are many animals at the ______________.

F Unscramble and write. 理一理，写出正确的单词。

1. o u g r n d a y p l

____

2. s p o t c e f i o f

____

3. p o r t i r a

____

4. n a b k

____

WORKBOOK

UNIT

8

Listen

LISTENING GOAL: Listen for Directions

听力训练目标：明确路径

Remember!
Directions tell how to go to a place. Listen for direction phrases like *go straight* and *turn left* to know how to go to a place.
路径能告诉我们如何去一个地方。注意听go straight和turn left等用于指路的短语。

A **Listen to the article *The National Museum of Korea*. Then put the pictures in order.** 听一听这篇文章，给图片排序。

A

☐

B

☐

C

☐

B **Think about *The National Museum of Korea*. What are some of the directions you hear? Choose ✔ or ✘.**
回想一下文章，你听到了哪些路径？判断正误。

1. To go to the children's museum, go across the street. ✔ ✘
2. To go to the children's museum, walk straight down the long hall. ✔ ✘
3. To go to the restaurant, go downstairs. ✔ ✘

C **Listen to *The National Museum of Korea* again. Choose Yes or No.**
再听一听文章，判断正误。

1. The National Museum of Korea is a small museum. **Yes** **No**
2. There are thousands of things in the museum. **Yes** **No**
3. It has a children's museum. **Yes** **No**
4. It has a room that teaches about old homes in Korea. **Yes** **No**
5. It has old clothing from Korea. **Yes** **No**
6. There is no place to eat at the museum. **Yes** **No**

D **Listen. Then read and choose the correct answer.**

听一听，读一读，并选择正确的答案。

1. Where does Yuki go every day at 8:00?

a. 
b. 
c. 

2. Where does Jack like to go on the weekend?

a. 
b. 
c. 

3. What is Etta's favorite place?

a. 
b. 
c. 

E **Complete the missing words.** 根据首字母提示，用本单元的重点词汇补全句子。

1. I can meet you at your a__________ after school.
2. What's your favorite food at this r__________?
3. My class visited an art m__________ last month.
4. I can walk to my s__________ from my home.

Speak

Remember!
Use action words to tell people where to go and what to do.
用动词告诉人们去哪里、做什么。

Circle the action words in the sentences. Then think of your own sentences with action words. Tell your partner.

把下列句子中的动词圈出来，然后用这些动词造句，并跟小伙伴说一说。

Turn right on Main Street.

Walk straight down the street.

WORKBOOK

UNIT 9

Listen

LISTENING GOAL: Listen for Setting

听力训练目标：明确背景

Remember!
The **setting** is *where* and *when* something happens.
背景就是事情发生的地点和时间。

A Listen to the story *Too Busy!*. What do you hear about? Choose ✔ or ✘. 听一听这个故事，你听到了什么内容？判断正误。

1. 

A girl writing an e-mail. ☐ ✔ ☐ ✘

2. 

A girl taking classes. ☐ ✔ ☐ ✘

B Think about *Too Busy!*. Choose ✔ or ✘. 回想一下故事，判断正误。

1. Jan is at home in the story. ☐ ✔ ☐ ✘
2. In the story, Jan goes to art class, swimming class, and a music lesson. ☐ ✔ ☐ ✘
3. Her classes are on Tuesday morning. ☐ ✔ ☐ ✘

C Listen to *Too Busy!* again. Choose the correct answer.
再听一听故事，选择正确的答案。

1. Where is Jan on Monday afternoon?
   ☐ a. In school. ☐ b. At the town center. ☐ c. At home.
2. What class does she have first?
   ☐ a. Music lesson. ☐ b. Swimming class. ☐ c. Art class.
3. How long does Jan have between her swimming class and her music lesson?
   ☐ a. Five minutes. ☐ b. Ten minutes. ☐ c. An hour.
4. What is Jan wearing at the end of the story?
   ☐ a. A coat. ☐ b. A baseball cap. ☐ c. Her swimsuit.

D Listen and write the word. Then choose the correct picture.

听一听，写出正确的短语，并选择相应的图片。

1. ______________________

☐ a

☐ b

2. ______________________

☐ a

☐ b

3. ______________________

☐ a

☐ b

4. ______________________

☐ a

☐ b

E Complete the sentences. 选一选，填一填。

go to swimming class	see a play	take an art class
have a music lesson	write an e-mail	practice violin

1. I ______________ to my grandmother in Mexico every week.
2. I ______________ in music class. I am getting very good!
3. Do you want to ______________ with me at the new theater?
4. We like painting so we ______________ after school.

F Unscramble and write. 理一理，写出正确的短语。

1. e p c r i a t c   i v l o n i

____

2. v e a h   a   s u c i m   s e o s n l

____

3. e s e   a   y l a p

____

4. i r e t w   n a   i m l a e -

____

WORKBOOK UNIT 10

Listen

LISTENING GOAL: Listen for Descriptions

听力训练目标：听清描述性词语

Remember!
A **description** tells how something looks, feels, sounds, and tastes.
描述性词语能告诉我们某物看起来、摸起来、听起来、尝起来是什么样的。

A Listen to the article *Go to Sleep!*. Then put the pictures in order.

听一听这篇文章，给图片排序。

A

☐

B

☐

C

☐

B Think about *Go to Sleep!*. How are different things described in the article? Choose ✔ or ✘.

回想一下文章，文章中是如何描述不同事物的？判断正误。

1. The weather is warm. ✔ ✘
2. The music is strange. ✔ ✘
3. The nap is long. ✔ ✘

C Listen to *Go to Sleep!* again. Choose Yes or No.

再听一听文章，判断正误。

1. It is always easy to fall asleep. **Yes** **No**
2. There is nothing you can do to help. **Yes** **No**
3. It can help to go for a walk. **Yes** **No**
4. It can help to get exercise. **Yes** **No**
5. Be quiet before you go to sleep. **Yes** **No**
6. Listen to loud music. **Yes** **No**

D Listen. Then read and choose the correct answer.

听一听，读一读，并选择正确的答案。

1. What does Dan want?

a. 

b. 

c. 

2. What does the girl want?

a. 

b. 

c. 

3. What do the children always do together?

a. 

b. 

c. 

E Complete the missing words. 根据首字母提示，用本单元的重点词汇补全句子。

1. We often g________________ in the park.
2. I like to l________________ before I go to sleep.
3. Let's m________________ car together.
4. Let's stay home this afternoon and p________________.

Remember!

Use description words like *hard*, *interesting*, and *small* before a person, place, or thing.

描述某人、某地或某物的时候，可以在前面加上描述性词语，比如hard、interesting、small。

Speak

Circle the description words in the sentences. Then think of your own sentence with description words. Tell your partner.

把下列句子中的描述性词语圈出来，然后试着用描述性词语造句，并跟小伙伴说一说。

I like to listen to loud music in the morning.

The math homework is hard.

WORKBOOK

UNIT

11

Listen

LISTENING GOAL:

Listen for What Is Similar

听力训练目标：听清相似之处

Remember!

Listen for words like *both*, *too*, and *also* to find what is **similar**.

注意听both、too和also等用于表示相似的词。

A Listen to the story ***Who Is Happy?***. What do you hear about? Choose ✔ or ✘. 听一听这个故事，你听到了什么内容？判断正误。

1.

Two boys. ☐✔ ☐✘

2.

Two girls. ☐✔ ☐✘

B Think about ***Who Is Happy?***. What is similar about the two people? Choose ✔ or ✘. 回想一下故事，这两个人有哪些相似之处？判断正误。

1. They are both 10 years old. ☐✔ ☐✘
2. They both are sons of kings. ☐✔ ☐✘
3. They are both happy. ☐✔ ☐✘

C Listen to ***Who Is Happy?*** again. Choose the correct answer.

再听一听故事，选择正确的答案。

1. How does James feel?

☐ a. Happy. ☐ b. Unhappy. ☐ c. Tired.

2. Whose hair does Ben brush?

☐ a. James' hair. ☐ b. His hair. ☐ c. His sister's hair.

3. What is in Ben's garden?

☐ a. Fruits and vegetables. ☐ b. Flowers. ☐ c. Only fruits.

4. Who takes care of Ben's garden?

☐ a. Ben. ☐ b. Ben's sister. ☐ c. James.

D Listen and write the word. Then choose the correct picture.

听一听，写出正确的单词，并选择相应的图片。

1. ____________________

☐ a

☐ b

2. ____________________

☐ a

☐ b

3. ____________________

☐ a

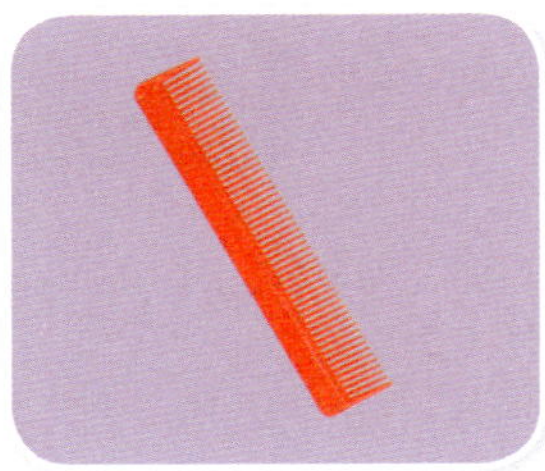

☐ b

4. ____________________

☐ a

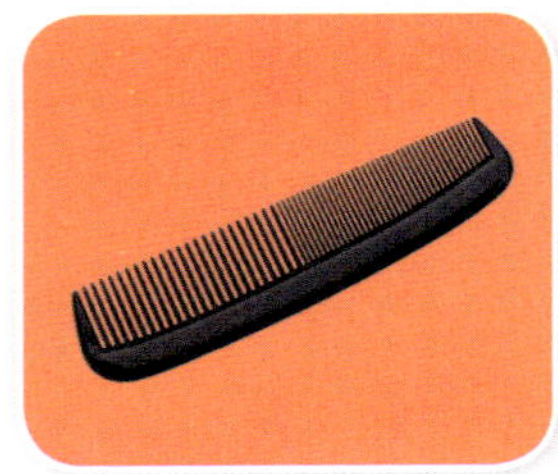

☐ b

E Complete the sentences. 选一选，填一填。

garden	comb	mirror	sink	brush	stairs

1. You look in the ____________________ too much!
2. I walk up lots of ____________________ to get to this class.
3. This ____________________ has many beautiful flowers.
4. You can get water at the ____________________.

F Unscramble and write. 理一理，写出正确的单词。

1. m o b c

____

2. u h r s b

____

3. s i a r t s

____

4. k i n s

____

WORKBOOK

UNIT

12

Listen

LISTENING GOAL:
Listen for What Is Different
听力训练目标：听清不同之处

Remember!
To find what is **different**, listen for words like *but*, *not*, and *unlike*.
注意听but、not和unlike等用于表示不同的词。

A Listen to the article *Rugs*. Then put the pictures in order.
听一听这篇文章，给图片排序。

A

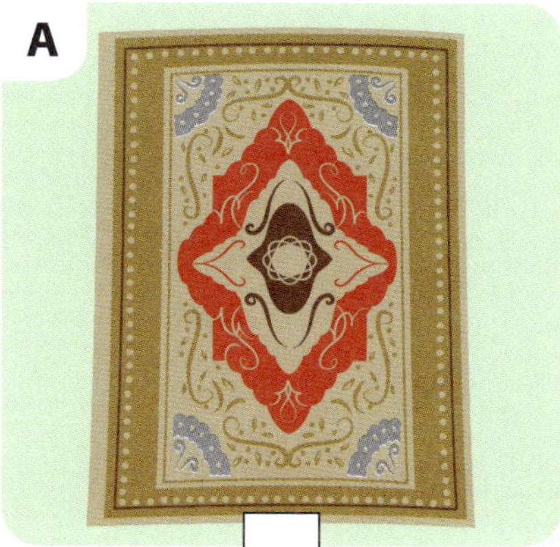

☐

B

☐

C

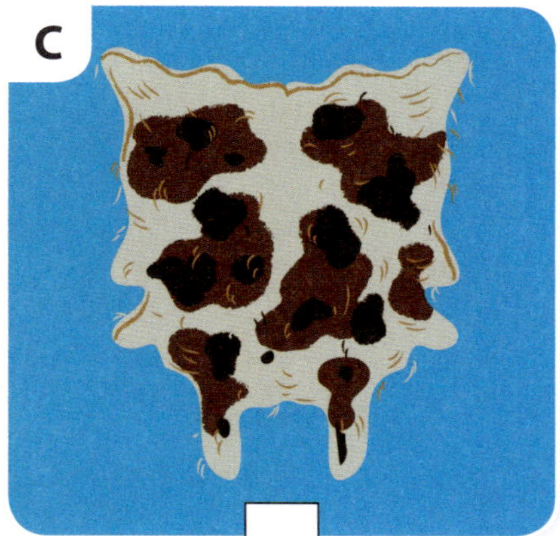

☐

B Think about *Rugs*. What things are different now than they were before? Choose ✔ or ✘. 回想一下文章，和之前相比，哪些事物不一样了？判断正误。

1. Rugs were hard to make, but now they are not. ✔ ✘
2. People used rugs, but now they do not use rugs. ✔ ✘
3. Rugs were only in rich people's homes, but now they are in many homes. ✔ ✘

C Listen to *Rugs* again. Choose Yes or No.
再听一听文章，判断正误。

1. First, people used parts of trees and grass to make rugs. **Yes** **No**
2. First, people used rocks to make rugs. **Yes** **No**
3. The rugs we know today started in the United States. **Yes** **No**
4. Some of the rugs we know today started in Egypt. **Yes** **No**
5. The rugs we know today started about 2,500 years before now. **Yes** **No**
6. Today, rugs are not hard to make. **Yes** **No**

D Listen. Then read and choose the correct answer.

听一听，读一读，并选择正确的答案。

1. What is the boy looking for?

a. 
b. 
c. 

2. Where is Beth sitting?

a. 
b. 
c. 

3. What does she like?

a. 
b. 
c. 

E Complete the missing words. 根据首字母提示，用本单元的重点词汇补全句子。

1. I'm making a cake in the o____________.
2. My sister is sleeping on the s____________.
3. The b____________ is in this bathroom.
4. The milk is in the r____________.

Remember!
To make a comparison, use phrases like *as well*, *similarly*, and *on the other hand*.
可以用as well、similarly和on the other hand来表示比较。

Speak

Circle the phrases *as well*, *similarly*, or *on the other hand* in the sentences. Then think of your own sentences and make comparisons. Tell your partner.

把下列句子中的 as well、similarly 和 on the other hand 圈出来，然后试着用这些单词和短语造句，并跟小伙伴说一说。

I live in an apartment, and my best friend does as well.

My home is near school. On the other hand, it is far from town.

Picture Dictionary

Write the key words.
写出重点词汇。

Unit 1

Unit 2

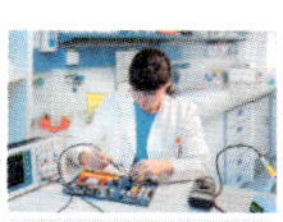

Unit 3

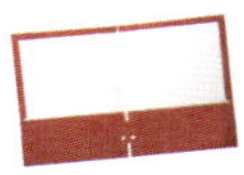

Unit 4

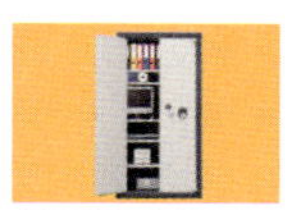

Unit 5

Unit 6

Unit 7

Unit 8

Unit 9

Unit 10

Unit 11

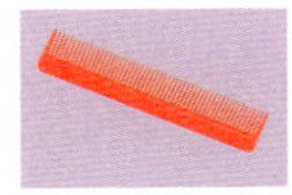

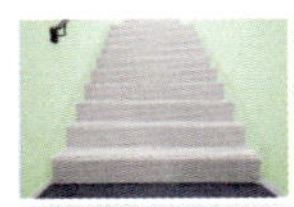

Unit 12

Answer Key

pp6–7

A
1. Answers will vary.
2. Answers will vary.

B
1. Most people work seven hours every day.
2. Answers will vary.

p8

B
1. a line from May to the driver
2. a line from Ann to the scientist
3. a line from Tom to the judge
4. a line from Alex to the news reporter

C
1. tailor
2. scientist
3. judge
4. musician
5. driver
6. news reporter

p9

A
1. bus
2. guitar, drums
3. pants, shirts, dresses

B
Answers will vary.
a. 2
b. 1
c. 3

pp10–11

A
a

B
1. Seven
2. judge
3. most important
4. musicians and the scientists
5. tailor

C
1. judge, a
2. driver, d
3. news reporter, c
4. scientist, b

D
1. judge
2. news reporter
3. tailor
4. driver
5. musicians
6. scientists

E
1. is a judge
2. are musicians
3. is a news reporter
4. are scientists

p12

B
1. mechanic
2. author
3. singer
4. cashier
5. engineer
6. astronaut

C
1. cashier
2. mechanic, engineer
3. astronaut
4. author, singer

p13

A
1. b
2. a
3. a

B
A
1. ✓
2. ✓
3. ×

pp14–15

A
1. Yes
2. No

B
1. a
2. a
3. b

C
1. a, engineer
2. b, cashier
3. a, mechanic
4. a, author

D
1. mechanics
2. engineer
3. astronauts
4. teacher

E
1. What do mechanics do?
2. What does an engineer do?
3. What do astronauts do?
4. What does a teacher do?

pp16–17

A
B

B
1. ×
2. ✓
3. ✓
4. ×

C
1. ✓
2. ×
3. ×
4. ✓

D
1. c
2. a
3. c
4. c
5. c

E
(1) judges
(2) news reporters
(3) mechanics
(4) scientist
(5) astronaut
(6) author
(7) singer

pp18–19

A
Underline:
Where are you from?
What school do you go to?
Who is your teacher?

B
Who: teacher
What: name, school
When: —
Where: from
Why: —

C
Answers will vary.

D
Answers will vary.

pp20–21

A
1. Answers will vary.
2. Answers will vary.

B
1. A tablet can have thousands of books.
2. Answers will vary.

p22

B
1. a line from Milo to the boy using a dictionary
2. a line from Anita to the girl using a workbook
3. a line from Ella to the girl who has a stapler and is using scissors
4. a line from Ben to the boy who has a folder and is using a calculator

C
1. dictionary
2. workbook
3. stapler
4. folder
5. calculator
6. scissors

p23

A
1. is
2. is
3. is not

B
A
a. 3
b. 2
c. 1

pp24–25

A
a

B
1. White
2. dictionary
3. every day
4. three
5. smiling

C
1. scissors, b
2. calculator, d
3. workbook, c
4. stapler, a

D
1. classroom
2. students
3. teacher
4. Asha and Abdul

E
1. has workbooks
2. has dictionaries
3. have calculators
4. have smiles

p26

B
1. drawer
2. flag
3. laptop
4. tablet
5. shelf
6. cabinet

C
1. flag
2. tablet
3. shelf, cabinet
4. laptop, drawer

p27

A
1. opinion
2. fact
3. opinion

B
A
1. ✓
2. ✓
3. ✗

pp28–29

A
1. No
2. Yes

B
1. a
2. b
3. b

C
1. a, drawer
2. a, cabinet
3. b, laptop
4. a, tablet

D
1. he
2. the teacher
3. they
4. the classmates

E
1. What is
2. What is
3. What are
4. What are

pp30–31

A
B

B
1. ✓
2. ✗
3. ✓
4. ✗

C
1. ✗
2. ✓
3. ✗
4. ✓

D
1. c
2. c
3. a
4. b
5. c

E
(1) calculator
(2) dictionary
(3) workbook
(4) stapler
(5) scissors
(6) cabinet

pp32–33

A
Underline: I don't think so. You're right.

B
1. dictionaries
2. calculators

C
Answers will vary.

D
Answers will vary.

pp34–35

A
1. Answers will vary.
2. Answers will vary.

B
1. They can shop with friends. They can try on the clothes. They can have fun.
2. Answers will vary.

p36

B
1. a line from Bess to the girl wearing a coat
2. a line from Lisa to the girl with a handbag and a swimsuit
3. a line from Tom to the boy wearing shorts and sneakers
4. a line from Jack to the boy wearing a baseball cap

C
1. swimsuit
2. shorts
3. baseball cap
4. handbag
5. coat
6. sneakers

p37

A
1. pink handbag
2. black coat
3. pants

B
A
a. 3
b. 1
c. 2

pp38–39

A
b

B
1. coats to swimsuits
2. baseball cap
3. shorts
4. white
5. money

C
1. sneakers, d
2. handbag, a
3. coat, b
4. swimsuit, c

D
1. No
2. Yes
3. Yes
4. No

E
1. No, don't
2. Yes, do
3. Yes, do
4. No, don't

p40

B
1. the thick book
2. the thin book
3. the heavy backpack
4. the light backpack
5. the dirty baseball cap
6. the clean baseball cap

C
1. heavy
2. light
3. clean, dirty
4. thick, thin

p41

A
1. ✓
2. ✗
3. ✓

B
A
1. ✓
2. ✗
3. ✓

pp42–43

A
1. Yes
2. No

B
1. b
2. a
3. a

C
1. a, dirty
2. b, heavy
3. a, thick
4. b, clean

D
1. blue shirt, too dirty
2. yellow shirt, too heavy
3. purple shirt, too thick
4. green shirt, too light

E
1. The blue shirt is too dirty.
2. The yellow shirt is too heavy.
3. The purple shirt is too thick.
4. The green shirt is too light.

pp44–45

A
B

B
1. ×
2. ✓
3. ✓
4. ×

C
1. ×
2. ✓
3. ✓
4. ×

D
1. b
2. b
3. c
4. a
5. c

E
(1) baseball caps
(2) sneakers
(3) heavy
(4) light
(5) shorts
(6) dirty

pp46–47

A
Underline: I prefer, I like, I like, I like

B
1. online, easy and fast
2. in stores, see things before she buys them

C
Answers will vary.

D
Answers will vary.

pp48–49

A
1. Answers will vary.
2. Answers will vary.

B
1. More than 37 million.
2. The special job is to push people inside subway trains.
   Answers will vary.

p50

B
1. a line from Jen to the girl at the airport with her father
2. a line from Prow to the girl at home reading a book
3. a line from Eva to the girl at the playground
4. a line from Dan to the boy at the zoo
5. a line from Ms. Gomez to the woman at the bank
6. a line from Mr. Awad to the man at the post office

C
1. home
2. zoo
3. post office
4. bank
5. airport
6. playground

p51

A
1. soup
2. school
3. zoo

B
B
a. 3
b. 2
c. 1

pp52–53

A
a

B
1. different
2. sad
3. do many things
4. before
5. leave

C
1. airport, d
2. playground, b
3. post office, a
4. home, c

D
1. playground, zoo, bank
2. playground, zoo, bank
3. post office, bank

E
1. go to the playground
2. go to the zoo
3. goes to the post office
4. go to the bank

p54

B
1. bookstore
2. restaurant
3. amusement park
4. school
5. museum
6. apartment

C
1. apartment
2. bookstore
3. amusement park, school
4. museum, restaurant

p55

A
1. ✓
2. ×
3. ✓

B
B
1. ×
2. ✓
3. ✓

pp56–57

A
1. Yes
2. No

B
1. b
2. b
3. b

C
1. b, school
2. a, bookstore
3. a, restaurant
4. b, amusement park

D
1. across from, restaurant
2. next to, bookstore
3. across from, park
4. behind, zoo

E
1. The museum is across from a restaurant.
2. The apartment is next to the bookstore.
3. The bookstore is across from the park.
4. The amusement park is behind the zoo.

pp58–59

A
A

B
1. ✓
2. ×
3. ✓
4. ✓

C
1. ×
2. ✓
3. ×
4. ✓

D
1. a
2. c
3. b
4. b
5. c

E
(1) amusement park
(2) zoo
(3) post office
(4) restaurant
(5) bookstore
(6) apartment

pp60–61

A
Underline: Go down, look for, turn right, Go straight down, Turn left

B
1. Go down this street.
2. Then turn right on Davis Street.
3. Go straight down Davis Street.
4. Turn left onto Elm Street.

C
Answers will vary.

D
Answers will vary.

pp62–63

A
1. Answers will vary.
2. Answers will vary.

B
1. It makes you smart.
2. Answers will vary.

p64

B
1. a line from Mia to the girl sees a play with her family
2. a line from Joe to the boy in a music class
3. a line from Dana to the girl practicing violin
4. a line from Joe to the boy writing e-mails
5. a line from Mia to the girl at an art class
6. a line from Ping to the boy in swimming class

C
1. see a play
2. practice violin
3. write an e-mail

4. have a music lesson
5. go to swimming class
6. take an art class

p65

A
1. time
2. time and place
3. place

B
B
a. 3
b. 2
c. 1

pp66–67

A
a

B
1. Friday
2. swimming class
3. seeing a play
4. Sunday
5. in the morning

C
1. take an art class, c
2. practice violin, d
3. see a play, a
4. write an e-mail, b

D
1. Friday
2. Saturday morning, Saturday night
3. Sunday

E
1. I'm sorry. I can't.
2. I'm sorry. I can't.
3. I'm sorry. I can't.
4. Yes, I can.

p68

B
1. play a board game
2. makes a model
3. takes a nap
4. listens to music
5. have fun
6. go for a walk

C
1. play a board game
2. make a model
3. listen to music, have fun
4. go for a walk, take a nap

p69

A
1. ✓
2. ×
3. ✓

B
A
1. ×
2. ×
3. ✓

pp70–71

A
1. No
2. Yes

B
1. b
2. a
3. b

C
1. a, take a nap
2. a, listen to music
3. b, make a model
4. a, go for a walk

D
1. go, nice
2. play, fun
3. listen, beautiful
4. take, short

E
1. Go for a nice walk.
2. Play a fun board game.
3. Listen to beautiful music.
4. Take a short nap.

pp72–73

A
A

B
1. ×
2. ✓
3. ✓
4. ×

C
1. ✓
2. ×
3. ✓
4. ×

D
1. b
2. a
3. c
4. a
5. b

E
(1) see a play
(2) write an e-mail
(3) have a music lesson
(4) go to swimming classes
(5) taking an art class
(6) have fun

pp74–75

A
Underline: interesting, hard, fun, small and easy, difficult

B
1. hard
2. easy
3. difficult

C
Answers will vary.

D
Answers will vary.

pp76–77

A
1. Answers will vary.
2. Answers will vary.

B
1. They moved around from one place to another.
2. Answers will vary.

p78

B
1. a line from Sara to the girl using a brush
2. a line from Joy to the woman in the garden
3. a line from Mark to the boy at the sink
4. a line from Leo to the man walking down the stairs

C
1. mirror
2. garden
3. brush
4. stairs
5. comb
6. sink

p79

A
1. small
2. five
3. vegetables

B
A
a. 1
b. 3
c. 2

pp80–81

A
a

B
1. another boy
2. small
3. brown
4. runs away from
5. mirror

C
1. garden, b
2. sink, a
3. comb, d
4. mirror, c

D
1. blue eyes
2. brown hair
3. small ears
4. a big nose

E
1. Peter and the boy both have blue eyes.
2. Peter and the boy both have a big nose.
3. Peter and the boy both have small ears.
4. Peter and the boy both have brown hair.

p82

B
1. refrigerator
2. sofa
3. bathtub
4. rug
5. oven
6. armchair

C
1. bathtub
2. rug
3. oven, refrigerator
4. sofa, armchair

p83

A
1. ×
2. ✓
3. ×

B
A
1. ✓
2. ×
3. ✓

pp84–85

A
1. Yes
2. No

B
1. b
2. a
3. b

C
1. a, refrigerator

2. b, rug
3. b, armchair
4. a, oven

D
1. fire
2. cold lakes or snow
3. wood chairs
4. water and an old piece of clothing

E
1. but in 1500 they used fire
2. but in 1500 they used cold lakes or snow
3. but in 1500 they used wood chairs
4. but in 1500 they used water and an old piece of clothing

pp86–87

A
A

B
1. ×
2. ✓
3. ×
4. ✓

C
1. ✓
2. ×
3. ✓
4. ×

D
1. a
2. a
3. a
4. c
5. a

E
(1) ovens
(2) refrigerators
(3) combs
(4) bathtubs
(5) mirrors
(6) gardens

pp88–89

A
Underline: Similarly, On the other hand, On the other hand

B
1. small living room
2. her own room
3. garden at the back of the home
4. big living room
5. not her own room

C
Answers will vary.

D
Answers will vary.

Workbook Answer Key

pp91–92

A
Answers will vary.

B
1. ✓
2. ✓
3. ×

C
1. a
2. c
3. b
4. b

D
1. tailor, a
2. judge, b
3. news reporter, a
4. driver, b

E
1. driver
2. musician
3. scientist
4. tailor

F
1. judge
2. driver
3. scientist
4. tailor

pp93–94

A
A. 1
B. 3
C. 2

B
1. ✓
2. ×
3. ×

C
1. No
2. Yes
3. No
4. No
5. Yes
6. Yes

D
1. b
2. a
3. b

E
1. singer
2. astronaut
3. mechanic
4. engineer

Speak
Circle: Who, What, Where
Answers will vary.

pp95–96

A
1. ×
2. ✓

B
1. ✓
2. ×
3. ✓

C
1. b
2. c
3. a
4. b

D
1. stapler, a
2. folder, a
3. calculator, b
4. scissors, a

E
1. workbook
2. calculator
3. scissors
4. folder

F
1. dictionary
2. stapler
3. folder
4. workbook

pp97–98

A
A. 2
B. 1
C. 3

B
1. ×
2. ✓
3. ×

C
1. Yes
2. No
3. Yes
4. Yes
5. No
6. Yes

D
1. c
2. a
3. c

E
1. flag
2. laptop
3. drawer
4. cabinet

Speak
Circle: You're right.
Underline: I don't think so.
Answers will vary.

pp99–100

A
1. ×
2. ✓

B
1. ✓
2. ×
3. ×

C
1. c
2. b

3. b
4. a

D
1. sneakers, b
2. coat, a
3. swimsuit, a
4. handbag, b

E
1. sneakers
2. swimsuit
3. handbag
4. coat

F
1. swimsuit
2. shorts
3. baseball cap
4. handbag

pp101–102

A
A. 2
B. 3
C. 1

B
1. ✓
2. ✓
3. ×

C
1. No
2. Yes
3. Yes
4. Yes
5. No
6. Yes

D
1. c
2. c
3. b

E
1. thin
2. clean
3. dirty
4. thick

Speak
Circle: like, because, prefers, because
Answers will vary.

pp103–104

A
1. ×
2. ✓

B
1. ×
2. ✓
3. ✓

C
1. b
2. a
3. a
4. c

D
1. post office, b
2. home, b
3. airport, a
4. zoo, b

E
1. bank
2. airport
3. home
4. zoo

F
1. playground
2. post office
3. airport
4. bank

pp105–106

A
A. 2
B. 1
C. 3

B
1. ×
2. ✓
3. ✓

C
1. No
2. Yes
3. Yes
4. Yes
5. Yes
6. No

D
1. b
2. c
3. a

E
1. apartment
2. restaurant
3. museum
4. school

Speak
Circle: Turn, Walk
Answers will vary.

pp107–108

A
1. ×
2. ✓

B
1. ×
2. ✓
3. ×

C
1. b
2. c
3. a
4. c

D
1. see a play, b
2. write an e-mail, a
3. take an art class, a
4. practice violin, b

E
1. write an e-mail
2. practice violin
3. see a play
4. take an art class

F
1. practice violin
2. have a music lesson
3. see a play
4. write an e-mail

pp109–110

A
A. 2
B. 1
C. 3

B
1. ×
2. ×
3. ✓

C
1. No
2. No
3. Yes
4. Yes
5. Yes
6. No

D
1. b
2. a
3. c

E
1. go for a walk
2. listen to music
3. make a model
4. play a board game

Speak
Circle: loud, hard
Answers will vary.

pp111–112

A
1 ✓
2. ×

B
1. ✓
2. ×
3. ×

C
1. b
2. c
3. a
4. a

D
1. mirror, b
2. brush, b
3. sink, a
4. comb, b

E
1. mirror
2. stairs
3. garden
4. sink

F
1. comb
2. brush
3. stairs
4. sink

pp113–114

A
A. 2
B. 3
C. 1

B
1. ✓
2. ×
3. ✓

C
1. Yes
2. No
3. No
4. Yes
5. Yes
6. Yes

D
1. c
2. a
3. b

E
1. oven
2. sofa
3. bathtub
4. refrigerator

Speak
Circle: as well, On the other hand
Answers will vary.

Audio Script

p7

B

Time at Work

Most people work about seven hours every day. This is 35 hours in a week, 140 hours in a month, and 1,680 hours in a year!

p8

A

driver
judge
musician
news reporter
scientist
tailor

B

1. May is a driver.
2. Ann is a scientist.
3. Tom is a judge. He is at the tailor's.
4. Alex is a news reporter. He is talking to a musician.

C

1. tailor
2. scientist
3. judge
4. musician
5. driver
6. news reporter

p9

A

1. A driver can drive a car, a truck, or a bus.
2. A musician plays the piano, the guitar, and the drums.
3. A tailor fixes pants, shirts, and dresses.

B

Take Me!

A taxi stops. Seven people run to it. They all want the taxi.
A man says, "Take me! I'm a judge. I have important work to do."
A woman says, "No, take me! I'm a news reporter. I have more important work to do!"
Another man says, "Please take me. My work is the most important."
The driver asks, "What is your job?"
The man says, "I'm a tailor. Without me, people do not have clothes."
The other people are two musicians and two scientists. They think the tailor is right. They leave.
The tailor smiles and gets into the taxi. "Let's go," he says to the driver.

p10

B

See script of *Take Me!*.

C

1. The judge works in a court.
2. The driver can drive a taxi.
3. The news reporter talks to people.
4. The scientist has an important job.

p11

D

See script of *Take Me!*.

p12

A

astronaut
author
cashier
engineer
mechanic
singer

B

1. The mechanic is working on a car.
2. The author is writing a book on her computer.
3. The singer is singing a song.
4. The cashier is giving the man money.
5. The engineer is helping to build a bridge.
6. The astronaut is in space.

C

1. The cashier works eight hours every day.
2. The mechanic and the engineer are fixing the problem together.
3. The astronaut has an exciting job.
4. The author and the singer are friends.

p13

A

1. The cashier works in a supermarket.
2. The musician plays a guitar.
3. The tailor fixes the pants on Tuesday.

B

What Job Do You Want?

Good morning, class. Today we are talking about jobs. What job do you want? There are so many! You can be a cashier, an author, a singer, and more! We have three people here to talk about their jobs.
Hi. I'm Jan. I'm a mechanic. What do mechanics do? They fix things like cars and bikes. They often work in garages.
Hello. I'm Bill. I'm an engineer. What does an engineer do? An engineer uses math and science to fix problems.
Hi, everyone. I'm Ellen. I'm an astronaut. What do astronauts do? We practice for a long time. Then we fly into space!
Thanks everyone! And what does a teacher do? Well, you already know the answer to that!

p14

B

See script of *What Job Do You Want?*.

C

1. An engineer uses math.
2. A cashier takes money from people.
3. I want a mechanic to fix my car.
4. Who is the author of that book?

p15

D

See script of *What Job Do You Want?*.

p16

A

Women at Work

Women can do any job! They are judges. They are news reporters. They are mechanics. Let's learn about some women with interesting jobs. These women are famous. Many people know them. Do you?
Yi So-Yeon is from South Korea. She is a scientist. She is also an astronaut. She was the first South Korean in space.
J. K. Rowling is a famous author. She is from England. She wrote the *Harry Potter* books. Children and adults around the world read her books.
Lata Mangeshkar is a singer. She is from India. She is about 90 years old. She was famous 50 years before now. She is still famous!
What can women do? Anything!

p17

D

See script of *Women at Work*.

E

See script of *Women at Work*.

p18

A

Meeting a New Friend

Hi. I'm Dan. What's your name?
Hi! I'm Allan. I'm from Watertown. Where are you from?
I'm from Watertown, too!
Really? What school do you go to?
I go to the Davis School.
So do I! Who is your teacher?
Mrs. Smith.

p21

B

Computers and Classrooms

Classrooms were very different 50 years before now. Then, children carried many books to school. Today, one tablet can have thousands of books!

p22

A

calculator
dictionary
folder
scissors
stapler
workbook

B

1. Milo is using a dictionary.
2. Anita is using a workbook.
3. Ella has a stapler and is using scissors.
4. Ben has a folder and he is using a calculator.

C

1. dictionary
2. workbook
3. stapler
4. folder
5. calculator
6. scissors

p23

A

1. All of the calculators in our classroom are blue.
2. The math workbook we use every day has 100 pages.
3. I think the math workbook we use is very difficult.

B

The First Day of School

It is the first day of school today! Welcome, students! I'm Mrs. White. I'm so glad you are here! I want to talk about the things to bring to class every day.
Please don't bring a dictionary, a stapler, or scissors. The classroom has these. I also have a workbook for you. But please bring your calculator and folder to school every day. And there is one more thing to bring to class every day—a smile! Smiles are great!
Do you have one today?
Oh, look at Asha! She has a smile. And look at Abdul. He has one, too!

p24

B

See script of *The First Day of School.*

C

1. Can you please give me the scissors?
2. I have a calculator in my desk.
3. The workbook is on the desk.
4. My teacher gave me a stapler to use.

p25

D

See script of *The First Day of School.*

p26

A

cabinet
drawer
flag
laptop
shelf
tablet

B

1. There is a stapler in the drawer.
2. There is a flag in the classroom.
3. There is a laptop on the desk.
4. The girl is holding the tablet.
5. The books are on the shelf.
6. The scissors are on the cabinet.

C

1. There is a flag in every classroom.
2. The student is using the tablet.
3. The scissors are on the shelf or in the cabinet.
4. The boy put his laptop in the drawer.

p27

A

1. I think my teacher is the best teacher in the world.
2. There are eight children in our class.
3. I think dogs are great.

B

Tim's Tablet

Tim can't find his tablet. His teacher looks up from her laptop. She thinks he looks sad. She asks, "What are you looking for?" Tim says, "I'm looking for my tablet."
The teacher counts. She says, "There are ten children and there are nine tablets. Oh, no! One tablet is missing!"
The students and the teacher look around the classroom for it. They look in the drawers. They look in the cabinet. They look on the shelf. They look behind the flag. But they do not find it. Tim says, "Oh!" The teacher says, "What, Tim?" Tim's face turns red. He says, "I know where my tablet is! It's at home!"

p28

B

See script of *Tim's Tablet.*

C

1. The child put his calculator in the drawer.
2. The books are in the cabinet.
3. The teacher is working on the laptop.
4. The tablet is on the table.

p29

D

See script of *Tim's Tablet.*

p30

A

Can I Use Your Dictionary?

The teacher asks Sal and Cora to be partners.
Sal says, "I'm glad you're my partner, Cora. You're so smart."
Cora says, "Thanks, Sal. You're so nice!"
Sal asks, "Can I use your calculator?" Cora says, "Sure!"
Then Sal asks, "Can I see your dictionary?" Cora says, "OK."
Soon, Sal says, "Can I look at your workbook?"
Cora says, "OK. But don't ask for my stapler or my scissors. There are some in the cabinet."
Sal says, "Thanks!"
Cora asks, "Why don't you have anything today?"
Sal says, "Oh. I do have everything." "You do?" asks Cora.
"Yes!" Sal says. "At home!"

p31

D

See script of *Can I Use Your Dictionary?.*

E

See script of *Can I Use Your Dictionary?.*

p32

A

The Important Things

What are the important things we use in class?
What do you think?
Calculators!
Really? Why?
They make math easier!
I don't think so. I don't think they are important. We can do math without them.
What do you think is important?
I think dictionaries are important.
You're right. Dictionaries are very important.

p35

B

Clothes Shopping

Shopping for things online is popular today. You can buy things quickly online. But more than 60% of people want to buy clothes in stores.
They can shop with friends. They can try on the clothes. Shopping with friends and trying on clothes can be a lot of fun!

p36

A

baseball cap
coat
handbag
shorts
sneakers
swimsuit

B

1. Bess is wearing a coat.
2. Lisa has a handbag and a swimsuit.
3. Tom is wearing shorts and sneakers.
4. Jack has a baseball cap.

C

1. swimsuit
2. shorts
3. baseball cap
4. handbag
5. coat
6. sneakers

p37

A

1. Jan likes the orange handbag, but she prefers the pink handbag.
2. Taro likes the red coat, but he likes the black coat more.
3. Asha doesn't like shorts. She prefers to wear pants.

B

Shopping with Mom

Mali and her mom are at a new store.
Wow, Mali! This store has so many things! It has everything from coats to swimsuits!
Look at these baseball caps! I want to buy one. And I want these sneakers!
Look at these red shorts, Mali. Do you like them?
No, I don't really like them. I like these blue ones more.
Look at these beautiful handbags, mom. Do you like the white one?
Yes, I do! There is a yellow one too. I don't really like it. I prefer the white one.
Well, we want lots of things. Do you have enough money for all of them?
No, I don't!

p38

B

See script of *Shopping with Mom*.

C

1. I wear sneakers almost every day.
2. Bring your handbag to the store.
3. Alec and I have the same coat.
4. I like your swimsuit.

p39

D

See script of *Shopping with Mom*.

p40

A

clean
dirty
heavy
light
thick
thin

B

1. Jose is reading a thick book.
2. Adam is reading a thin book.
3. Inez has a heavy backpack.
4. Erin has a light backpack.
5. Minh has a dirty baseball cap.
6. John has a clean baseball cap.

C

1. The backpack is heavy.
2. The handbag is light.
3. Are the sneakers clean or dirty?
4. Your hair is thick. It isn't thin.

p41

A

1. I like these shorts because they're my favorite color—red.
2. I prefer the big shirt because it's more comfortable.
3. I prefer the thick coat because it keeps me warm in cold weather.

B

The Little Brother

Marco's little brother Gil is eating a banana. He gets it all over his blue shirt.
Marco's mother says, "Gil's shirt is too dirty. Please put a clean one on him."
Marco takes a yellow shirt out of the drawer. Gil says, "No, I don't like that shirt!"
Marco asks, "Why not?"
Gil answers, "Because it's too heavy."
Marco tries a purple one, but Gil says it's too thick. Marco shows Gil a green shirt, but again, Gil says, "No!"
Marco asks, "Why don't you like this one?"
Gil says, "Because it's too light."
Marco takes off his thin, red shirt and puts it on Gil. Gil smiles and is happy now.

p42

B

See script of *The Little Brother*.

C

1. The pants are dirty.
2. The dumbbell is heavy.
3. The coat is thick.
4. The shoes are clean.

p43

D

See script of *The Little Brother*.

p44

A

What Clothes Do They Wear?

Baseball players wear special hats, shoes, and clothes. The players wear these things because they help them play well.
They wear baseball caps because these hats keep the sun out of their eyes.
They wear special kinds of sneakers called cleats. They prefer cleats because cleats help them run. They also help them not fall down.
Players wear special pants and a shirt. These clothes are not heavy. They are very light. This helps them play and run. Baseball players do not wear shorts. Why not? Because their legs get very dirty when they play!

p45

D

See script of *What Clothes Do They Wear?*.

E

See script of *What Clothes Do They Wear?*.

p46

A

I want new sneakers. I want to ask my mom to take me shopping.
You can ask her to buy you sneakers online.
I don't really like shopping on the computer.
Why not?
I prefer to shop in stores.
Really? Why?
Because I like to see things before I buy them. And I like going shopping. Which do you prefer?
I'm not sure. I think I like shopping online because it's easy and fast!
That's true!

p49

B

City Life

Tokyo is a very big city. It has over 37 million people! Many, many people ride the Tokyo subways. There are people with special jobs. Their job is to push people inside the subway trains!

p50

A

airport
bank
home
playground
post office
zoo

B

1. Jen is at the airport with her father.
2. Prow is at home.
3. Eva is at the playground.
4. Dan is at the zoo.
5. Ms. Gomez is at the bank.
6. Mr. Awad is at the post office.

C

1. home
2. zoo
3. post office
4. bank
5. airport
6. playground

p51

A

1. Adam's family eats dinner together every night. To start, they have soup. After that, they have meat and a vegetable.
2. Every day, Lin does the same thing. To start, she goes to school. After that, she goes to the playground.
3. Yesterday, Jack visited the zoo. After that, he visited his grandmother.

B

Fun Trip

Hanna and Rosa are pen pals. They write each other every month. Hanna lives in Mexico. Rosa lives in Spain. Hanna is visiting Rosa for the first time.
Rosa and her family meet Hanna at the airport. At first, Hanna feels sad. She thinks about home. But on her first day, they do so many things, Hanna forgets to be sad! To start, they go to the playground. After that, they go to the zoo. Rosa's mom goes to the post office but before that, they go with her to the bank.
Some things are different in Spain. Others are the same. When the week is over, Hanna doesn't want to leave!

p52

B

See script of *Fun Trip.*

C

1. The airport is crowded.
2. Let's go to the playground after school.
3. I want to go to the post office today.
4. My brother is at home now.

p53

D

See script of *Fun Trip.*

p54

A

amusement park
apartment
bookstore
museum
restaurant
school

B

1. You can buy books at the bookstore.
2. You can get food at the restaurant.
3. You can have fun at the amusement park.
4. You can learn at the school.
5. You can see art at the museum.
6. You can live in the apartment.

C

1. The apartment is very large.
2. Where is the bookstore?
3. I want to go to the amusement park after school today.
4. After we go to the museum, let's go to a restaurant.

p55

A

1. To get to my apartment, go straight on Elm Street.
2. To get to the restaurant, turn left on Green Street.
3. To get to the museum, walk down Rose Street.

B

Come Over!

Hi, this is Carla. I can't answer my phone. Please leave a message after the beep.
Hi, Carla. This is Marco. My birthday is on Friday. Can you come to my birthday party on Friday after school?
Let's meet at my apartment. To get there from school, walk down Main Street. Go straight and walk to the museum. The museum is across from a restaurant. Turn left at the museum. The apartment is next to a bookstore. The bookstore is across from a park. My parents want to take us to an amusement park. It is behind the zoo. After that, they want to take us to a restaurant. We are getting ready for a fun party! I hope you can come!

p56

B

See script of *Come Over!.*

C

1. I am at my school now.
2. Let's go to the bookstore.
3. I was at a restaurant last night.
4. There is an amusement park in my town.

p57

D

See script of *Come Over!.*

p58

A

Things to Do in Town

Today is Dana's birthday. She wants to go to the amusement park or the zoo. But her mother gives her things to do in town. "To start, go down the street to the post office with this letter. After that, turn right and go to the restaurant next to the bookstore to get food." Dana does these things. Then she goes home. When she goes into her apartment, she hears "Surprise!" It's a party! Her friends are here! Dana's mother takes the box from her. She opens it. It's a birthday cake! Dana's mother says, "I wanted you to be busy. We wanted to get ready for the party!"

p59

D

See script of *Things to Do in Town.*

E

See script of *Things to Do in Town.*

p60

A

Excuse me. Can you give me directions to the post office?
Sure. Go down this street. Look for a school.
OK. Then what?
Then turn right on Davis Street.
Is the post office on Davis Street?
No. Go straight down Davis Street to the corner of Davis and Elm streets.
OK.
Turn left onto Elm Street. The post office is on Elm Street between a bookstore and the museum.
OK. Thank you very much for your help.

p63

B

Music Is Good for You!

Do you have music lessons? Do you listen to music a lot? Then there's good news for you! Scientists think playing and listening to music makes you smart! It helps you learn better and more quickly.

p64

A

go to swimming class
have a music lesson
practice violin
see a play
take an art class
write an e-mail

B
1. Mia often sees a play with her family.
2. Joe has a music lesson every Saturday.
3. Dana practices violin every day.
4. Joe writes e-mails every day.
5. Mia takes an art class on Tuesday.
6. Ping goes to swimming class on Monday.

C
1. see a play
2. practice violin
3. write an e-mail
4. have a music lesson
5. go to swimming class
6. take an art class

p65

A
1. It's 7:30 in the morning and Jim is tired.
2. It's 9 o'clock and Jenna is having fun at the amusement park.
3. The students are learning new words in class.

B
Come to My House
Dan sees his friend Ray on the school playground on Friday. Dan asks, "Can you come to my house after school?"
"I can't," says Ray. "I go to swimming class after school. Then I practice violin. Maybe Saturday? Can you play on Saturday?"
Dan says, "I have a music lesson that morning, and then an art class. At night I'm seeing a play. Maybe Sunday?"
"Yes, Sunday is good!" says Ray. "8 o'clock?" "Yes!" says Dan.
On Saturday, Dan writes Ray an e-mail. "See you tomorrow at 8 o'clock."
On Sunday at 8 o'clock in the morning, Ray goes to Dan's house.
"Why are you here now?" Dan asks.
"We're meeting at 8 o'clock." Ray says, "It is 8 o'clock. Oh! We didn't say morning or night!"

p66

B
See script of *Come to My House*.

C
1. I take an art class every Saturday afternoon.
2. I practice violin for an hour each day.
3. Do you want to see a play with me tonight?
4. I want to write an e-mail before I go to sleep.

p67

D
See script of *Come to My House*.

p68

A
go for a walk
have fun
listen to music
make a model
play a board game
take a nap

B
1. Seth and Ari play a board game.
2. Fadil makes a model.
3. Ella takes a nap.
4. Jing listens to music.
5. Sue and Amira have fun.
6. Jess and Sharon go for a walk.

C
1. Ben and his parents play a board game every night.
2. I want to make a model of my favorite car.
3. My older sister and her friends like to listen to music and have fun.
4. After they go for a walk, they want to take a nap.

p69

A
1. Sleep is good for you.
2. They are listening to beautiful music.
3. That board game is a lot of fun to play!

B
Tips for Busy Kids
Today kids are busy with school, after-school activities, sports, and friends. But it is not good to always be busy. It can make you tired. When you get very tired, you can even get sick. Do you want to feel good? Then it is important to have some quiet time every day. For example:
Go for a nice walk.
Smell the pretty flowers and listen to the little birds.
Play a fun board game with a friend.
Make a model in a quiet room.
Listen to beautiful music.
Take a short nap. Sleep is good for you.
And most importantly—have fun and be happy!

p70

B
See script of *Tips for Busy Kids*.

C
1. You look tired. You should take a nap.
2. I listen to music every night before I sleep.
3. We are making a model.
4. Come on. Let's go for a walk.

p71

D
See script of *Tips for Busy Kids*.

p72

A
A Place for Fun
Welcome to our town center building! It's Monday afternoon, and there is so much to do here. You can see a play in our beautiful theater or write an e-mail in our quiet computer room. You can have a music lesson in the music room or go to swimming classes in our big, new pool! Let's visit our after-school art class. Ten students are taking an art class here this afternoon. Let's talk to Ryan. Ryan, can you tell us what you think about this art class?
It's great! We do really interesting projects. And every week we have fun.
Thanks, Ryan! Come down to the town center building and have some fun with us!

p73

D
See script of *A Place for Fun*.

E
See script of *A Place for Fun*.

p74

A
Hi. I'm Greg. I love making interesting models. It takes a lot of time and hard work. But it is fun work.
I started making them when I was five. Those models were small and easy because they only had a few pieces.
I make much more difficult models now. They have many small pieces!

p77

B
A Time Before Houses
People did not always live in houses. Thousands of years before now, people did not even live in one place. They moved around from one place to another. Some people still live this way now. Their homes are tents.

p78

A
brush
comb
garden
mirror
sink
stairs

B
1. Sara is looking in the mirror and using a brush.
2. Joy is in the garden.
3. Mark is at the sink with a comb.
4. Leo is walking down the stairs.

C
1. mirror
2. garden
3. brush
4. stairs
5. comb
6. sink

p79

A
1. Sofia lives in a small house. Daniel lives in a small house too.
2. Aisha has five people in her family. Jess also has five people in her family.
3. We grow vegetables in our garden, and you do too.

B
The Mirror
Peter's family moves to a new house. The first morning there, Peter uses the sink to brush his teeth. Then he uses his brush and comb.He looks up and shouts "Aaaah!" There is another boy in his house! They both have blue eyes. And they both have a big nose and small ears. And the boy also has brown hair! Peter runs down the stairs and through the garden. He comes back to the house later. Slowly, he walks into the bathroom. He sees the boy again! The boy looks scared too. Peter pushes it away. When he does, his hand hits the mirror. Peter laughs. The boy is him!

p80

B
See script of *The Mirror.*

C
1. I like your garden.
2. Where is the sink?
3. I have a black comb, too.
4. That is a small mirror.

p81

D
See script of *The Mirror.*

p82

A
armchair
bathtub
oven
refrigerator
rug
sofa

B
1. The refrigerator is open.
2. The girls are on the sofa.
3. The bathtub is in the bathroom.
4. There is a rug under the sofa.
5. There is a chicken in the oven.
6. The mother is sitting in the armchair.

C
1. Ed doesn't have a bathtub in his house.
2. That rug is very nice.
3. We use our oven and refrigerator every day.
4. We have the same sofa and armchair!

p83

A
1. We don't have a sofa, but we have an armchair.
2. Jing has a sister, not a brother.
3. John lives in a big house. Unlike John, Al lives in a small house.

B
Then and Now
Our homes are nice. When we are tired, we sit in an armchair or a sofa. We have rugs. They look nice. We have ovens to cook food. We have refrigerators to keep food cold. But it was different in the year 1500. Unlike now, people did not have armchairs or sofas. They sat on wood chairs. They did not have ovens. They cooked food over fire! They did not have refrigerators. They used cold lakes or snow as their refrigerator! They did not have bathtubs. They washed with water and an old piece of clothing. It was a very different time!

p84

B
See script of *Then and Now.*

C
1. Put the food in the refrigerator.
2. That is a beautiful rug.
3. The armchair is comfortable.
4. The food is in the oven.

p85

D
See script of *Then and Now.*

p86

A
Just Like Us
People in Egypt 5,000 years before now were different from us in many ways. Their ovens were very different. They didn't have refrigerators. But they were similar to us too. We want to look good. This was true for them too! We use combs. They used them too. They used parts of trees for their combs. There were no bathtubs, but they washed themselves in the river. They also used mirrors. We have gardens, and they did too. In many ways, they were just like us!

p87

D
See script of *Just Like Us.*

E
See script of *Just Like Us.*

p88

A
Welcome Home
by Hoshi Ito
My home is new. My family just moved to it last year. In some ways, it is like our old home. There was a garden at the back of our old home. Similarly, there is a garden at the back of my new home. On the other hand, some things are different in the new home. In the old home, there was a very big living room with big windows. The living room in our new home is small. On the other hand, I have my own room for the first time in the new home. I'm very excited about that!

p91

A
The Zookeeper's Problem
A driver comes to the zoo. He has a new animal in his van. It is a cute panda. All the people want to see it. A news reporter is there too. The driver opens the door. The panda does not come out.
The zookeeper brings her food. But the panda won't come out.
The zookeeper asks nicely. But the panda won't come out.
Then, a visitor says, "Let me help."
The zookeeper says, "You? What do you do? How can you help?"
The visitor says, "I'm a musician. Watch."
The woman takes out her guitar. She begins to play beautiful music.
The panda comes out! The people clap!

C
See script of *The Zookeeper's Problem*.

p92

D
1. tailor
2. judge
3. news reporter
4. driver

p93

A
Mechanic to Astronaut
Andrew Jay Feustel was a mechanic. He fixed cars. He liked his job. He was good at his job. But he had other dreams. He dreamed about space. He wanted to be an astronaut.
Andrew studied very hard. Then he took a test to be an astronaut. He got a good score! Now he is an astronaut. He works with scientists. He fixes things in space. He loves his job and

he is great at his job. He can work on the International Space Station and fix things!

C
See script of *Mechanic to Astronaut*.

p94

D
1. The author writes many books.
2. The cashier has a dollar.
3. The engineer works in a factory.

p95

A
Before Calculators
We use many tools in the classroom. We use scissors to cut. We use a dictionary to learn new words. We use a calculator to do math. What did people use to count before there were calculators? In Egypt, China, and other countries, people used a tool called an abacus. This tool had sticks. There were seven beads on each stick. People moved the pieces of wood, and with this tool, it was easy to count. But now we have calculators. It is easier to do math with a calculator!

C
See script of *Before Calculators*.

p96

D
1. stapler
2. folder
3. calculator
4. scissors

p97

A
The Visit
Jen and Al are from Brazil. Their class is learning about China. They open a laptop. They type in "China." Suddenly, Jen and Al feel tired. They fall asleep and they wake up and see a Chinese flag. They look around. They are not in their class. They are in a class in China! The students run to Jen and Al and ask questions about Brazil. Al wants to show pictures of his country. He types "Brazil" into the laptop.
Al and Jen fall asleep again. They wake up in their own class! They say, "China was very interesting. But that was odd!" They put the laptop back in the cabinet for the day!

C
See script of *The Visit*.

p98

D
1. Each child in class has a tablet.
2. There is a flag on the wall of the classroom.
3. The books are in the drawer.

p99

A
Clothing Then and Now
Think about the clothes you wear. Do you think people liked the same clothes in the year 1890?
No!
They liked big hats. Today, most people do not wear big hats. They wear small hats like baseball caps.
In 1890, the coats were long. Most coats were black. Today people wear long and short coats. They wear blue, yellow, and green coats!
Are you ready for a surprise? At that time, there were no sneakers! People used shoes and boots. There were no special shoes for sports.
Some people prefer the clothes of 1890. Many like the clothes we have today. What do you prefer?

C
See script of *Clothing Then and Now*.

p100

D
1. sneakers
2. coat
3. swimsuit
4. handbag

p101

A
The New Coat
Amal goes shopping for a new coat with his father.
His father points to one and says, "This is nice. Why don't you try it on?"
Amal tries it on and says, "I don't like it because it's too heavy."
His father laughs and points out that Amal put the coat on over his own coat. Amal takes off his coat and tries it again.
"Hey," Amal says, "It's nice and light." Amal looks in the mirror and says, "But this one is dirty."
His father doesn't understand. He says, "It's not dirty." Then Amal's father looks at the mirror, laughs again, and says, "The mirror is dirty— not the coat!"

C
See script of *The New Coat*.

p102

D
1. Jan's new book is very thick.
2. Taro's sneakers are dirty.
3. My pants are clean.

p103

A
Where Is It?
"I have gold!" Rabbit tells Wolf.
Wolf says, "Really? Where is it?"
Rabbit answers happily, "It is in a safe place." Wolf wants the gold. To start, when Rabbit goes, Wolf looks all over her home. But he can't find the gold anywhere.
After that, Wolf has an idea. Maybe Lion is keeping the gold safe! So Wolf goes to the zoo and looks all around Lion. But, again, he doesn't find anything. Lion roars and Wolf runs away.
A few days later, Wolf sees Rabbit again. Wolf asks, "Rabbit, where is the safe place for your gold?"
"Don't you know?" asks Rabbit. "The bank, of course!"

C
See script of *Where Is It?*.

p104

D
1. post office
2. home
3. airport
4. zoo

p105

A
The National Museum of Korea
Do you want to learn about Korea? Go to the National Museum of Korea! It is a very large museum. There are thousands of things to look at there.
There is even a children's museum in it! How do you get to the children's museum? There is a long hall in the museum. Walk straight down the hall. It goes to the children's museum. There are different rooms in the children's museum.
One teaches kids about old homes in Korea. Go around the corner and see a room with old Korean clothing.
Are you hungry? Go downstairs. There is a restaurant. Or go right outside of the museum to find a cafe!

C
See script of *The National Museum of Korea*.

p106

D
1. Yuki goes to school every day at 8 o' clock.
2. Jack likes to go to the bookstore on the weekend.
3. Etta's favorite place is the amusement park.

p107

A

Too Busy!

Jan is busy. It is Monday afternoon. She takes an art class at the town center. After art class, she goes to a swimming class at the pool. She gets into her swimsuit quickly and goes to the pool. After the swimming class, Jan has a music lesson. She only has five minutes to get there! She gets out of the pool. Then she runs to her music lesson. She walks into the room. Her teacher and the three other students look at her. The teacher asks, "What are you wearing?" Jan looks down. She is still wearing her swimsuit!

C

See script of *Too Busy!*.

p108

D

1. see a play
2. write an e-mail
3. take an art class
4. practice violin

p109

A

Go to Sleep

Sometimes it's hard to fall asleep. You want to fall asleep, but you can't! What can you do?
These things can help:
Go for a nice walk before you go to bed. Move your body around, and get some exercise. Feel the cold weather. Look at the stars. Be quiet before you go to bed. Don't listen to a loud TV or loud music. Listen to beautiful music before bedtime. It can help you feel very sleepy. All of these can help you sleep better at night.
But maybe you still have trouble sleeping.
That's OK. You can take a long nap the next day!

C

See script of *Go to Sleep.*

p110

D

1. Dan wants to take a nap.
2. Let's play a board game.
3. The children always have fun together.

p111

A

Who Is Happy?

James and Ben are both 10 years old.
James is the son of a king. His home is at the top of many stairs. It has a beautiful garden of flowers. People bring James food. They brush his hair with a gold brush. But James is unhappy. He has nothing to do.
Ben is a tailor's son. There are no stairs to Ben's home. But there is a garden at Ben's home too. It is small. It has only fruits and vegetables. Ben takes care of the garden. He brushes his sister's hair. Ben has many things to do. He is happy.
Working and helping others makes people happy.

C

See script of *Who Is Happy?*.

p112

D

1. mirror
2. brush
3. sink
4. comb

p113

A

Rugs

Look under your armchair or sofa. Do you see a rug? Rugs have a story. First, people used animal hair to make rugs. They also used trees and grass. These rugs were warm places to sit and sleep. The kind of rugs we know today are different.
These rugs started in Egypt, the Middle East, and Asia about 2,500 years before now. They were beautiful, but they were hard to make. They were only in rich people's homes.
Today, rugs are not hard to make, and they are in many homes. They are soft and feel nice to sit on. Rugs make a house look beautiful!

C

See script of *Rugs*.

p114

D

1. Where is the refrigerator?
2. Beth is sitting in the armchair.
3. I like this rug.